THE NEW
LONG POEM
ANTHOLOGY

THE NEW
LONG POEM
ANTHOLOGY

EDITED BY
SHARON THESEN

COACH HOUSE PRESS · TORONTO

For the selection and introduction, © Sharon Thesen, 1991

Published with the assistance of the Canada Council and the Ontario Arts Council.

Canadian Cataloguing in Publication Data

Main entry under title:

The New Long Poem Anthology

ISBN 0-88910-407-7

1. Canadian poetry (English) - 20th century.*
I. Thesen, Sharon, 1946-   .

PS8279.N4 1991   C811'.5408   C91-093228-3
PR9195.7.N4   1991

Cover photograph: Thaddeus Holownia
"Abandoned Boats," Dartmouth, Nova Scotia, March 1986
Courtesy: Jane Corkin Gallery, Toronto

ACKNOWLEDGEMENTS

I'd like to thank Michael Ondaatje for having the foresight to put together the first *Long Poem Anthology* in 1979. Thanks also to Robin Blaser, Phyllis Webb and George Bowering, for the conversations. – S. T.

The following selections were originally published by Coach House Press and are reprinted in this anthology with the kind permission of the authors:

Blaser, Robin, "The Moth Poem," from *The Long Poem Anthology,* © 1979 by Robin Blaser.

Bowering, George, "Elegy Nine" and "Elegy Ten," from *Kerrisdale Elegies,* © 1984 by George Bowering.

Brand, Dionne, "No Language Is Neutral," from *No Language Is Neutral,* © 1990 by Dionne Brand.

Kiyooka, Roy, "Pear Tree Pomes," the complete text of *Pear Tree Pomes,* © 1987 by Roy Kiyooka.

McKinnon, Barry, "Sex at Thirty-One," from *The the,* © 1980 by Barry McKinnon.

Nichol, bp, "Inchoate Road," from *The Martyrology Book 6 Books,* © 1987 by bpNichol. Reprinted with the permission of his estate.

Ondaatje, Michael, "Tin Roof," from *Secular Love,* © 1984 by Michael Ondaatje.

Acknowledgement for the other poems in this volume is made as follows:

Dewdney, Christopher, "The Cenozoic Asylum," from *Predators of the Adoration,* © 1983 by Christopher Dewdney. Used by permission of the Canadian Publishers, McClelland & Stewart, Toronto.

The other is emerging as the necessary prerequisite for dialogues with the self that clarify the soul's heart and deepen the ability to love. I place myself there, with them, whoever they are, wherever they are, who seek to reach themselves and the other through the poem by as many exits and entrances as possible.

bpNichol, 1966

CONTENTS

SHARON THESEN
INTRODUCTION

Since 1979, when Coach House Press published the first Canadian long poem anthology and Michael Ondaatje in his introduction was perplexed by the lack of recognition accorded the long poem – "the most interesting writing being done by poets today" – the form has become so well-established that to include even a sample of the best long poems written in the last decade would require many more volumes. So I begin by stating that this anthology is not meant as an encyclopedia of the Canadian long poem but rather as a continuation of Ondaatje's work in 1979 and a record of my own pleasure in reading poems that in many different ways, occasions and structures are "long."

The absences are many and troubling, and for the dozens of writers of long poems whose work does not appear here, I round up the usual reasons: limited space and the whims of taste, as well as the need to include several long poems of historic importance ("The Moth Poem," "Naked Poems") as well as work by innovative long-poem writers such as Robert Kroetsch, bpNichol, Daphne Marlatt and George Bowering. And then a genie hovers about with its own shaping agenda, so that one notices in the end that the poems chosen seem largely to be meditational, lyric / anti-lyric, processive and attached to a sense of beauty and desire problematic to their writers. Such bias could as easily be attributed to the fact that many narrative, documentary and "persona" long poems tend to run to book length. The poems in this volume, with a few exceptions, are either parts of longer works or are extended, sequential, serial, lengthy, longish or otherwise self-limiting poems. In some sense, all poets are composing the "long poem" of their writing lives; in another sense the "true" long poem would go on forever – or at least for the duration of the poet's life. Robin Blaser's *The Holy Forest* and bpNichol's *The Martyrology* are examples of life-long poems, pieces of which appear in this volume. Similarly, Robert Kroetsch's *Completed Field Notes*, from which "Delphi: Commentary" was taken, are completed only for now. As Fred Wah has pointed out, however, poems such as Zukovsky's *A*, Olson's *The Maximus Poems* and Nichol's *The Martyrology* "maintain continuity and delay or minimize endings. For most long poems ... the ending cannot be delayed for long."

Long poems belong by practice and definition to what Ezra Pound called the "prose tradition" in poetry; that is, their tendency to a narrative sense of the passage of time drives them by and into history beyond the capacities and preoccupations of the lyric. The long poem in Canada is often a way of handling that distrust of the "poetic" associated with the lyric voice, seen as a falseness, a colonizing wish overlaid upon the real: so Kroetsch's "Seed Catalogue," a taxonomy of the limits of cultivated beauty in a land represented as blank space even on fairly recent maps. Dionne Brand, speaking as an immigrant, also speculates in "No Language Is Neutral" that "In another place, not here, a woman might touch something between beauty and nowhere, back there and here, might pass hand over hand her own trembling life," and it is not clear what countries "here" and "there" refer to besides the countries of language and history, "the hard gossip of race." So also the rewriting of outlaw "myths" to a tangle of events both true and not true, dependent always upon who is speaking them: Ondaatje's "Billy the Kid," Cooley's "Bloody Jack," MacEwen's "T. E. Lawrence," Jiles's "Jesse James." Other "myths" are poets and writers whose canonical significance is at once acknowledged, parodied and undermined in such virtuoso plays of intertextuality as Stephen Scobie's "Dunino" and George Bowering's "Kerrisdale Elegies," two of which, traced over the famous ninth and tenth elegies of Rilke's series, are published here.

But for many long-poem poets, the form offers simply an opportunity to continue, to accumulate, to push into new territories or to draw them out seductively, slowly, patiently. The erotics of the long poem find unforgettable expression in the first lines of Robert Kroetsch's essay "For Play and Entrance": "In love-making, in writing the long poem – delay is both – delay is both technique and content." The long poem is a place where union and separation, entering and exiting (and existing) can go on, unencumbered by the pressure of lyric closure. Marlatt's "Touch to My Tongue" is such a poem, breathtaking in the extravagance of its continuous erotic moment. "Gyno-Text", by Lola Lemire Tostevin, literally recapitulates conception, its mystery both intact and revealed. And in "The Cenozoic Asylum," Christopher Dewdney tracks the course of natural history as a cosmology of pulsation and desire palpable in the shine of a leaf or the contours of a landscape.

Observing that "Robert Kroetsch views the impulse toward the long poem as a resistance to end and Frank Davey sees it as a desire to continue," Fred Wah proceeds in his essay "Making Strange" to delineate the forces that keep long poems going on, including the looping ways in which they pause in order to continue. And it is easy to see how both the resistance to end and the desire to continue (or as Bowering has it, "running from doom and longing for fortune") are the essential experiences of life itself. The poetic diary or *utaniki* is a long-poem sensibility that bpNichol has acknowledged as a major influence on *The Martyrology*. *Utaniki* tracks a section of the writer's life as a discontinuous yet continuing story of consciousness. It avoids the demands of autobiographical rationalization by a process of estrangement: the poet is, after all, frequently on a journey to "far towns," as Basho had it. Diana Hartog's "Oasis" is a familiar image and yet a mirage: the poet's experience of a desert night-world of fearsome clarity. Nichol's "Inchoate Road" is the road of writing, the way there; and "there" is a destination forever postponed. Journeying is as often "back" as "to" and long poems are frequently a form for charting a complex of stories that precede and inform one's own, as Fred Wah does in "This Dendrite Map: Father / Mother Haibun." The light jabs of mortality in "Sex at Thirty-One" (as distinct from sex at twenty-one, let alone at forty-one: a complete mystery) are the preoccupations of Barry McKinnon on dark winter nights in the far town of Prince George, B.C. And in *Pear Tree Pomes* Roy Kiyooka writes the diary of his garden's pear tree through a round of seasons and briefly beyond the moment of its destruction. In its concern with time and its paralleling of a history of love with the the demise of the pear tree, Kiyooka's poem can be firmly placed in the *utaniki* tradition.

When the Long-Liners' Conference was held at York University in 1985, there was a lot of talk about trying to "get the long poem on the curriculum." To whatever degree the long poem now appears as a classroom text, it is nevertheless widely acknowledged by writers and scholars as a vital and powerful form in postmodern Canadian writing. An anthology of prairie long poems has appeared; *The Malahat Review* sponsors an annual long-poem contest; the annual bpNichol / Therafields chapbook prize allows for even more recognition.

The long poems excluded from this anthology could themselves constitute several more anthologies. I regret the omission of book-length poems such as Peter Dale Scott's *Coming to Jakarta*, John Thompson's *Stilt Jack*, Fred Wah's *Music at the Heart of Thinking*, Dennis Cooley's *Bloody Jack*, Yolande Villemaire's *Quartz and Mica*. Each of these poems deserves study, as do the various and beautiful long, sequential or suite poems written by Don McKay, D. G. Jones, Stuart MacKinnon, Mary di Michele, Douglas Barbour, Bruce Whiteman, Andy Suknaski, Margaret Atwood, Colin Browne, Dorothy Livesay, Stephen Scobie, Dennis Lee, Paulette Jiles, Lorna Crozier and many others. As the long poem continues to transform and be transformed by issues in contemporary poetics, it will evolve new ways of seeing, imagining and holding our selves' lives, for as the poem goes, so does the self, "opening," as bpNichol had it, "as wide as possible while struggling for precision through a meditational process of accumulation."

SHARON THESEN, 1991

ROBIN BLASER

THE MOTH POEM

for H. D.

A Literalist

the root and mirror
of a plant
               its shape
and power familiar
iris

the light is disturbed by
the boxwood   leaves
shining
               rosemary
green, unblossoming
(the earth is too damp)

the eye catches
almost a tune

the moth in the piano
wherein
               unhammered
the air rings with

an earlier un
ease of the senses
disturbed (by Mrs. Arpan,
wife of a sailor

The Literalist

the wind does not move on
to another place

bends into,
as in a mirror,
                    the
breaking

the moth in the piano
will play on
frightened wings brush
the wired interior
of that machine

I said, "master"

Between

the morning face of
turns you who
turn

      a complete
interior furniture
flecked with
the children
of the moth
         how
loud you are
against glass

the strings of / play on

this
    that
        now scattered

The Borrower

the one loved is
holding a moth
thin, metallic dark
model with a triangular
crest

what's out and secret
spills
the wind dries
moves on

               the interior
of his body
                  red water
with white threads
                      the bone
a ghost of his thigh
                  pale
blue gut holding the shit

highway

Awake

in the dark morning you are circled
by loss of sleep   you lean forward
from the balcony to see the moth
dying in the window   swept by
still wings

loose pieces of air fall
cold and catch your eyelids

the words don't fit you

your back is a mirror   your
hand a bowl holding the musical
moth

Supper Guest

leaning over the white
linen which casts

a pale light
over his face,

we are not deprived
the white bowl

must shine
behind our words,

leave us
in a fire of clouds

the tin flowers
the castles

which drift out
of our mouths

whitely
in the cold air,

fantômes
de sentiments

magic juices
on the eyelids,

so it is
what is met

a white moth carries its moth-body
trying the way into corners

The Medium

it is essentially reluctance   the language
a darkness, a friendship, tying to the real
but it is unreal

the clarity desired, a wish for true sight,
all tangling

"you" tried me, the everyday which
caught me, turning the house

in the wind, a lovecraft   the political
was not my business   I could not look

without seeing the decay, the shit poured
on most things, by indifference, the personal

power which is simply that,   demanding a friend
take dullness out of the world   (he doesn't know
his lousy emptiness)   I slept
in a fire   on my book bag, one dried wing

of a white moth   the story is of a man
who lost his way in the holy wood

because the way had never been taken without
at least two friends, one on each side,

and I believe my dream said one of the others
always led   now left to acknowledge,

he can't breathe, the darkness bled
the white wing,   one   of the body

of the moth that moved him, of the other
wing,   the language is bereft

O-friend

it was time you came
this night   you were NO

man attached to this opposite,
seen through a gate   or handed

his hat   you were as held
in a vase   orange calendula

and hot pink geraniums in blue
glass   that tropism

made you laugh   and the room,
is it possible you do not exist

separate from that glow
when I turned the flashlight

on the door?   who is there
who came dragging his

bag of tears? and remained
invisible   the whine is

not in me   is not part
of the moth who escapes

the cold in my electric
blanket   I suppose

I heard the dark and
with the craft wrought

against memory, it should
have been of no consequence

but the bones breathe, that
frame of what is contained,

opposites   the Sorrows sit
nearby surely,   cracking

their paws   once, the I
came on the Lady Bugs' home

at the foot of a redwood
they swarmed in heaps

their shells and loosened wings
flew in the wind of my steps

and once, Proteus, the goldfish,
jumped out of his bowl,   left

the color of dried orange peel
and so it is a turn of the wheel

you left   a kind of music,
la-de-da   and stink

in the air   held close
with the invisible rose,

O-imaginarie-in-knowledge

Invisible Pencil,

one does not willingly take the honey
sweet plant,   the words are lost, the
holy language simultaneous with this speech,

and flatteries, this participation in mirrors,
turns from the streets of some minds
one follows another man who kissed his shadow

now a moth flies overhead to the floorlamp,
stops my reading the *Death of Virgil,*
form fixed and mute,   one element

participates in his travels
more than another,   watery source
as if the hometown river flowed

into the room and out of the heart

Atlantis

draws back from the shine on the water,
the crumbling pieces flow unattached

the cement patches, the fit of the dark
streets around the towers   the wet

touches   spring a trap in personal
history,   interior, riotous   smokers

of poetry bathe among the ruins,
slip off the rocks,   green and

waking with weeds of the sea
the technical movement is made

by the water harp   in *moth-time*
the waves lift the bunched-up

newspaper, full of foam,   then
looking up, I see it run back, *defecate*

to a pure transparency,   the castles,
the lighted cliffs

Atlantis

the light of it, as he felt himself perish,
the *riotous moth,*   back and forth

there is a spilled glass of water, an ocean
spreading on the table

under the shine on the water, the pieces
flow, unattached   it will be that

horseplay the mouth takes for milk,   the
fit of the rivers around the books,

ashtrays, yellow apple and pomegranate
here   the web falls, sticky,   holding

the forehead   the apparent violence
bathed in,   a key to this privacy

he leaned over his poem   a piece
of blood fell out of his head   dazzling

clock sounds, the riotous moth, happiness
and this habit of light   *the sad soul*

wanders about *a spirit like an image*
this image enters the ghost
                              ly sent iment

My Dear ——

                    we end with you
circling your garden, allowing
the officials to lead you in,
trivial and cheap at Gump's,
the worthless mention of Snellgrove,
Pomeroy, Hack divided, phony last
suppers, démodé drips on the California
landscape, fake spooks in the upper
right hand corner of the orange machine,
brief agony for the dining room wall
at a price,   you, coming to
ignore this language

which is colored, takes in slime, is
some center where one is helpless
even to oneself,   flowers of the mouth,
it is smoke, alive only in the
car lights,   is stationary,

considered as paint full of secrets   flows,
still on the wall like a moth   until
it is pushed, then separating

with an outward stammer, officially
immortal,   to feed itself,   the final
thing
            somebody else's idea

Paradise Quotations

the stairs did not creak, but the snow did
I fixed the telescope and looking through I saw
a stag
        on the way back I saw the traces
of blood, but no longer believed in their
existence

first in translucent lymph with cobweb-threads
the Brain's fine floating tissue swells, and spreads

the marble hand, probably from its contact
with the uncharmed harp, had strength to
relax its hold and yield the harp to me

nerve after nerve the glistening spine descends
the red Heart dances, the Aorta bends

the white rose of Eddy-foam, where the stream
ran into a scooped or scalloped hollow of the
Rock in its channel   this Shape, an exact
white rose, was for ever overpowered by the
Stream rushing down in upon it, and still
obstinate in resurrection it spread up into
the Scallop, by fits and starts, blossoming
in a moment into a full Flower

through each new gland the purple current glides,
new Veins meandering drink the refluent tides

for here would be the moonbeams on the ice,
glittering through a warrior's breastplate
      whenever a breeze went by, it swept the old
men's heads, the women's beauty, and all the
unreal throng, into one indistinguishable
cloud   ever-anxious crowd

edge over edge expands the hardening scale,
and sheathes his slimy skin in silver mail

it   it   it   it

a white shadow there on the glass,
the white T-shirt   turns that

are no longer an end
less meaning   leans forward to the

shaping, to find it, a flutter of the
darkness, but it ducks back

from the open slit of the window,
a cinnamon moth enters
and amorous, the lamp takes
it   came from the back

garden planted with pale flowers
that might show in the dark   it
mocked, tripped, then toted its
image, having no past, unprepared

the *moth-kiss* has two languages,
the one everyday, dusty, habitual,
and part delight, the other
an *unexpended myth* washes against

the glass, to be abstract, untied
by the friendship,   the moment caught

Salut

you, priest, must know why you strike
tearing, teasing in that silly personality
if you fell, it is the rain falling down
the hanging pot of ivy, each leaf a-light
the grass of my eyes holding to a point,
the dew,   the spring

the piano, it was a gift, a promise of a debt
of music   it was moth under the strings,
frantic to escape, played
   wings eyed like an owl came to the lamp

the cold has come, the moths have gone,
white, grey, cinnamon and one rested
in the sun, wine purple wings, yellow
edged, tacked with the wind's changes,
careened, then, taking flight, hid
in the fig tree

the circles   the moon, the stars, the
plants and below, under the earth, the sun
between the earth and the moon, a tone
beyond that, the lyre

asleep, the four oval paintings, stories alive,
the artist of the moth, his foot upon the lion's
paw of the table   there is no storm in the
glass, only the white edge of a sleeve, the
form, nothing beyond that I   I

further asleep, there are petunias, white, red,
rose and night, zinnias, red, violet, orange, roses,
silver and yellow, nasturtiums, yellow, pansies, blue,
hollyhocks, pastel and waxy, violets, lilacs, sumac,
castor-bean flowers, flags, purple, white, brown

what is the day,   what is the charm, she, her
madness, yours, musical poplars, the mind
nearly destroyed by the presences, the fine
points which have no beginning

restless jewels   she is from the-light on the rails,
a-light running miles to a point   she is
in the house, an old railroad coach placed
on foundations by the railbed   among golden rod
and hop vines   she stands in the middle
of the room with arms outstretched, to protect
the bat, which caught, brown and velvet, she
puts to her breast against the yellow apron

this flower which is no flower   this new
land   the day filled with invisible princes,
Dr. Dolittle, the moon, the flow of rain
lighting the ivy   there is no meaning here,
there is all meaning here   Fran and Stan
laughing, the blue glass is $9.00, the Houssin
Isadora Duncan, looking more like Rodin's Balzac
is $350   there is nothing here but an intense,
interior monologue with moments of color, forms
flowing toward beloved plants   the cost has
been high   when all the world is loved by the
daimon of mediocrity,   you, priest,

must know why you strike

C

D

♭E

G

A

♭B

B

D

The Translator: A Tale

first, the pool of water   just waking my arms hold
it   the circle of the cold morning air

last night's coffee spoon sticks to the drainboard
under it the clear print of a brown moth, made of sugar,
cream, coffee with chicory, and a Mexican spoon of blue
and white enamel

The ashtray is full and should be emptied before work-
ing that translation,   *Attis ran to the wooded pastures*
of the weavers of gold, the shadowy place, where as if a
bee stung his brain, he took a flint knife and let the
weight of his cock and balls drop from him,   so

when she felt her limbs lose her manhood, still with
fresh blood spotting the ground, she grabbed the drum
with snowy hands,   beating the polished hide with soft
fingers,   she rose to sing to her companions

the mound of cigarette butts moves,   the ashes shift,
fall back on themselves like sand,   startle   out of
the ashes, awakened by my burning cigarette, a brown
moth noses its way,   takes flight

GEORGE BOWERING

KERRISDALE ELEGIES

NINE AND TEN

Elegy Nine

The laurel bush grows enormous, nearly obliterating
the front steps and pouring its dark waxy leaves over
into the porch.

             I never sit there, though I could,
there are two Yankee Stadium seats on the porch.

I could sit there,
             reading poetry,
                    imitating

that robust companion,
                reading, perhaps, Mallarmé.

                          But they said I had
                            [to be

human,
        running from doom,
                longing for fortune.

Half the beautiful ones I have known are gone.

My longing is not for happiness –
                            that only proves
your days are leaving one by one.

                        Not even to see
what's in the mail this morning.

                        Not just
to get the sap running,
                    any bush can do that.

Because here this once I can be bound to
meaning,
             because it looks as if the world wanted me,
the disappearing neighbourhood needs my step.

I will be the first to go,
                          my one chance spent so quick.

One for you, too.
                    One chance to offer to the world
meaning.

          No second stanza to develop,
                                   you'd better
write a good first verse.

                    But you could have
died in the womb,
                  you did get this one blank page.

No eraser can undo your visit.

On my dresser upstairs you'll find a limestone pebble
I brought across the sky from a cliffside path
at Duino.

       I'll leave it here when I go,
                          along with
everything else.

       Just so,
            we run over the earth,
carry pieces of it in our hands,
               so we squeeze it
and demand meaning,
           we urge it to resemble our heart.

I brought eleven pieces of Duino home with me
and gave away ten,
           but think the one I retain
is really me,
       I havent given away anything.

I want to keep it in my bedroom forever.

Importun
Vent qui rage!
Les défunts?
Ça voyage.

Our words will stay – maybe – pebbles to tell of our pain,
the hard path we had to walk for a few years,
the long long moments of love,
                              or trying to love.

Things that could never be told,
                              so we gave words instead.

Stranger yet the nights we got out from under the street lamps,
could see the still,
                    stars at least,
                              feel
a little homesick.

                    Then we knew enough to come back empty.

No one brings a stone away from that home.

I came back in the morning,
                                eyes half open,
                                                to say
chestnut tree, laurel bush, cherry, front porch, eyes
open,
                to tell bird, window, lover, determined insect
happily burrowed in the earth round these gladiola.

To count them and bind them to life,
                                        to praise
them and energize the earth.

                                Those lovers in the car
are seduced not by each other but by secret earth
filled with proper desire for transfiguration.

                                That I
should say such a word in a poem.

                                They kiss
and feel the press of more than their own flesh,
they are happy to add their hot hands
to the never-ending shaping and praising of the world.

The trick of the dance is in following,
                                now the words,
allegro,
                now the contrary beat of the glossy leaf.

It is time to speak now,
                          to say the words that are
ready,
          to name the world we can still see,
                                        the leaves
depart their tree but the tree is here.

                              Speak, praise,
before the tree is gone with your going,
                              before
you become act without words.

                    It is no bed of roses,
being dead.
              Your silent blood is a message
from a dying messenger.
                    It is filled with words
your tongue can move into sound,
                          words your neighbourhood deserves.

The ghastly dead will never applaud your imitation of them,
your beautiful silence.

                    They wrote the book on silence.

They own the rights to invisible meaning.

                                        Show them
something made of earth,
                            bring out the foot stool
your father made in high school shop,
                            a necklace
your grandmother bought from a Haida fisherman;

things,
        made by hands and real as their names.

Say look at these marvels,
                    we did these, we
have eyes and hands,
                    our best poet said
the optic heart must venture.

                    They will stare
and applaud,
            as you did,
                    watching
the father and son on Queretero Street bending cane
to make chairs till the light fell up the walls.

Praise our things.

            They are innocent in our hands,
the sweet pain of Archie Shepp's tenor saxophone
lives for fingers and ears,
                        show them how we love,
how we grace the earth a horn is fashioned from.

The earth,
            how it requires us to live,
                              how it
desires to become us.

            How the ash trees along Larch Street
turn to me for their life,
                  to this ephemeron in running shoes.

All right,
        I hear you,
                I know you want to grow again
in another soil,
           if that's what I am.
                    To disappear
and live again in me.
             All your seasons have been
practice transformations.
             Is this possible?
                  Am I
going mad in Kerrisdale?
              Lightning and love,
if Spring comes again she will nod her head
in my heart –
       all right, I agree,
              you may die
and move in.
       I will give you a new name.

Another mouth to feed,
           what's that?
                I was a child,
God knows what I'll be tomorrow.
              Now I'm a new
husband,
     now I am something like two.

Elegy Ten

Est-ce toi, Nomade, qui nous passeras ce soir aux
rives du réel?

If I endure, when this ghastly truth has passed my eyes,
may I raise music to my dead family in the dark.

Lift this light horn and play a song I know but
have never learned,
                    fingers touching keys I cannot see
through tears I always knew were there.

                            Remember
when we were kids,
                how we wept and secretly
loved our tears?

            How wise we were,
                      children see
where they are going.
               How their parents and teachers
mock them,
           drilling, memorizing happy little songs.

In November the wind slides in from the sea
and eats at our faces.

                    We should smile and bow,
it is the air of a sweet and terrible quartet.
                                   Precious

agony.

       How we threw away half our lives
waiting like cows for better weather.

                          Suffering
is our winter of bare branches,
                         our secret abode.

So we walk like strangers in Kerrisdale streets,
feet sore in our shoes,
                    forehead aching from our
squint in the rain.

                    The slapping of car tires on wet street
resounds from walls and fences,
                                engines droning
on the next block,
                    noise folding into noise till
we hear nothing but the occasional climbing DC-10.

We are inside an enormous overturned empty cup.

The shingled Anglican church across 37th Avenue,
highrises filled with perfumed widows asleep,
cosy women's-wear shoppes on 41st,
                                all
could be flattened by one ghost stepping off
the road between the stars.

But all winter the parks will be green,
                              and in the parks
the shades of kids and dads,
                              running from base to base,
throwing balls,
              falling over dogs,
                              dutifully dropping
ice cream wrappers in trash barrels,
                              a lot of
shouting under trees filled with the shades of leaves.

(And across the field,
                    real estate plotters wondering
who to bribe,
              to grab all that green and call it
undeveloped.)

        Later in the bars on Hastings Street
dads and others down that lovely gold stuff,

                get gold

into their veins,

        find something to laugh about,

                avoid

falling chairs,

      and convince themselves they'll never die.

They'll get into a car in two o'clock rain but never die.
There's a traffic cop called Real Death but he's
on the other side of town,

           where strangers are assholes.

In the after-hours joint full of smoke children are playing guitars,
lovers are propped against their alien clothes,
the toilet flushes endlessly behind the thin wall.

A slightly drunk dad is amazed by the different beauty
of a thin young woman with sorrow in her eyes.

It takes a while to determine that she's here alone,
she doesnt have a car,
                        her thin shoulders implore, they
demand to be nuzzled.
                        She's too good for this place.

With a stupid remark he begins a conversation
whose intention is to find out whether he can afford
to take her home.

                    Even when she says she lives
on the road between the stars,
                                he finds cause
to think she's lovely.
                        But he also thinks that he
is stupid.

                    He buys another tequila screwdriver
and drifts,
                    and drives home to early morning Kerrisdale,
his windshield wipers crossing the wet snow in her eyes.

Like an old singing branch I call out,
                              but only
those who died in their first cantos follow her home.

Dying girls and dying boys,
                         they follow her home.

Girls envy her rich diaphanous comet tail dress,
boys hold her sweet cold hand,
                              walking from her car.

They are at last near the abode where the immortals are
all as beautiful as she,
                   the ghastly company,
                                   refusing
a closing couplet.

All as beautiful,
    and all with sorrowful eyes;

            one
more proximate than the rest converses with the young
visitor,
    the newly dead.

       We were all strong like you,
she says,
    all like you fit to be praised.

We made this place by our coming here,
          we worked
with what was left.
     We drew from our own eyes
the molecules laid on one another for this city.

She signalled to some others who joined them
as they walked about the streets.

             Look, she said,
at the tall apartments held aloft by faint sighs
drifting from the mouths of lorn pensioners in their rooms.

She gestured to the tall trees,
                   their brilliant limbs
fashioned from tears,
                the bordering flowers grown only
out of pain.

         Every back yard is prowled by cats
with eyes of sharp grief,
              fixed on birds
that fill the trees and rooftops with songs of their agony.

Only in a shaded chamber of his stilled mind
does this youth realize he has been strolling through
Kerrisdale
        and around the earth.

He does not recognize me as he passes with his escort,
nor do I see him.

        Only the breeze fails in saying
what it half wants me to hear,
                on the shores of the real.

When light slips up the walls and away,
                                      they lead him
to the graveyard on 41st Avenue,
                             eerie tautology
in a neighbourhood of unseen grannies,
                                  glistening
with decreation.

                 And as all the light races skywards
to settle as tight calligraphy on the black dome above,
they walk with him to the school ground on the hill
and bid him read.

                He sees,
                       it is an unfolded road map,
ghastly brother to the grid he's made of his life in secret,
a call to greater travel,
                    a total denial of abode.

When he lifts his eyes to look there,
                                he knows
he is truly gone.

A new ghost,
                his half-wrinkled brain out of sync,
he cannot see the neighbourhood clear.

                                But she
tells the narrative of the newly dead to its hero —

a black bird in the dark night descends like the last leaf
from the chestnut tree outside his unseen house,
past his open unseeing eyes,
                        past his alert ear,
offering a song where no bird sings at night on earth,
a short poem of unwelcome comfort,
                                a direction
to read where reading erases the words
line by line,
            street by street.

Till the last page opens onto the earth
beyond his darkened acres,

                above invisible branches.

Every star becomes a coal as he reads it,

                figures
turning to ashes:

          the Archer, the Scribe,
the one he's always called the Infielder, to the south
the Triestino,

        quickly followed by the Coyote,
the Wine Glass, Erato, the three-armed Saguaro.

Last to go,

        drawing his reluctant gaze,
the clear white diamonds of the Number Nine.

Love is yearning for the stars,
                                        they will
come on again inside the committed dead.

                                        Time falls from him
as he follows his vaporous guides as far as they may go.

You have walked along this street,
                                        their beautiful leader tells him,
most of your life,
                    you recognize that dark doorway,
and that.

            In the morning the shopkeepers
will not see you
                    but feel your presence in the wind,
make satisfied jests about the season's immediate cold.

She looks at him a last time with her lorn eyes
and he is alone.

He walks out of Kerrisdale a last time,
                                  not turning to look
but seeing it all.

              The sun rises unknown to him.

His feet no longer feel the pavement.

                              If he did cry out,
none would hear.

But as he goes,
        his going lifts our eyes;
                we see
a little more from time to time.

             November sun
on the maple's cushioning moss,
          bamboo canes
across the corner of a window,
        he leaves us this;

we rush to call it meaning.

We see every thing's entry,
                          the robins that sing,
                                    la la,
the muscular dog that trots down our street the first time,

each quick appearance is a farewell.

The single events that raise our eyes and stop our time
are saying goodbye, lover,
                         goodbye.

DIONNE BRAND

NO LANGUAGE

IS NEUTRAL

No language is neutral. I used to haunt the beach at
Guaya, two rivers sentinel the country sand, not
backra white but nigger brown sand, one river dead
and teeming from waste and alligators, the other
rumbling to the ocean in a tumult, the swift undertow
blocking the crossing of little girls except on the tied
up dress hips of big women, then, the taste of leaving
was already on my tongue and cut deep into my
skinny pigeon toed way, language here was strict
description and teeth edging truth. Here was beauty
and here was nowhere. The smell of hurrying passed
my nostrils with the smell of sea water and fresh fish
wind, there was history which had taught my eyes to
look for escape even beneath the almond leaves fat
as women, the conch shell tiny as sand, the rock
stone old like water. I learned to read this from a
woman whose hand trembled at the past, then even
being born to her was temporary, wet and thrown half
dressed among the dozens of brown legs itching to
run. It was as if a signal burning like a fer de lance's
sting turned my eyes against the water even as love
for this nigger beach became resolute.

There it was anyway, some damn memory half-eaten
and half hungry. To hate this, they must have been
dragged through the Manzinilla spitting out the last
spun syllables for cruelty, new sound forming,
pushing toward lips made to bubble blood. This road
could match that. Hard-bitten on mangrove and wild
bush, the sea wind heaving any remnants of
consonant curses into choking aspirate. No
language is neutral seared in the spine's unravelling.
Here is history too. A backbone bending and
unbending without a word, heat, bellowing these
lungs spongy, exhaled in humming, the ocean, a
way out and not anything of beauty, tipping turquoise
and scandalous. The malicious horizon made us the
essential thinkers of technology. How to fly gravity,
how to balance basket and prose reaching for
murder. Silence done curse god and beauty here,
people does hear things in this heliconia peace
a morphology of rolling chain and copper gong
now shape this twang, falsettos of whip and air
rudiment this grammar. Take what I tell you. When
these barracks held slaves between their stone
halters, talking was left for night and hush was idiom
and hot core.

When Liney reach here is up to the time I hear about.
Why I always have to go back to that old woman who
wasn't even from here but from another barracoon, I
never understand but deeply as if is something that
have no end. Even she daughter didn't know but only
leave me she life like a brown stone to see. I in the
middle of a plane ride now a good century from their
living or imagination, around me is a people I will
only understand as full of ugliness that make me
weep full past my own tears and before hers. Liney,
when she live through two man, is so the second one
bring she here on his penultimate hope and she
come and sweep sand into my eye. So is there I meet
she in a recollection through Ben, son, now ninety,
ex-saga boy and image, perhaps eyes of my mama,
Liney daughter. I beg him to recall something of my
mama, something of his mama. The ninety year old
water of his eyes swell like the river he remember
and he say, *she was a sugar cake, sweet sweet*
sweet. Yuh muma! that girl was a sugar cake!

This time Liney done see vision in this green guava season, fly skinless and turn into river fish, dream sheself, praise god, without sex and womb when sex is hell and womb is she to pay. So dancing an old man the castilian around this christmas living room my little sister and me get Ben to tell we any story he remember, and in between his own trail of conquests and pretty clothes, in between his never sleeping with a woman who wasn't clean because he was a scornful man, in between our absent query were they scornful women too, Liney smiled on his gold teeth. The castilian out of breath, the dampness of his shrunken skin reminding us, Oh god! laughing, sister! we will kill uncle dancing!

In between, Liney, in between, as if your life could
never see itself, blooded and coarsened on this
island as mine, driven over places too hard to know
in their easy terror. As if your life could never hear
itself as still some years, god, ages, have passed
without your autobiography now between my stories
and the time I have to remember and the passages
that I too take out of liking, between me and history
we have made a patch of it, a verse still missing you
at the subject, a chapter yellowed and moth eaten at
the end. I could never save a cactus leaf between
pages, Liney, those other girls could make them root
undisturbed in the steam of unread books, not me,
admiring their devotion, still I peered too often at my
leaf, eyeing the creeping death out of it and giving up.
That hovel in the cocoa near the sweet oil factory I'll
never see, Liney, each time I go I stand at the road
arguing with myself. Sidelong looks are my specialty.
That saddle of children given you by one man then
another, the bear and darn and mend of your vagina
she like to walk about plenty, Ben said, *she was a
small woman, small small.* I chase Ben's romance as
it mumbles to a close, then, the rum and coconut
water of his eyes as he prepares to lie gently for his
own redemption. *I was she favourite, oh yes.*
The ric rac running of your story remains braided in
other wars, Liney, no one is interested in telling the
truth. History will only hear you if you give birth to a
woman who smoothes starched linen in the wardrobe
drawer, trembles when she walks and who gives birth
to another woman who cries near a river and
vanishes and who gives birth to a woman who is a
poet, and, even then.

Pilate was that river I never crossed as a child. A woman, my mother, was weeping on its banks, weeping for the sufferer she would become, she a too black woman weeping, those little girls trailing her footsteps reluctantly and without love for this shaking woman blood and salt in her mouth, weeping, that river gushed past her feet blocked her flight ... and go where, lady, weeping and go where, turning back to face herself now only the oblique shape of something without expectation, her body composed in doubt then she'd come to bend her back, to dissemble, then to stand on anger like a ledge, a tilting house, the crazy curtain blazing at her teeth. A woman who thought she was human but got the message, female and black and somehow those who gave it to her were like family, mother and brother, spitting woman at her, somehow they were the only place to return to and this gushing river had already swallowed most of her, the little girls drowned on its indifferent bank, the river hardened like the centre of her, spinning chalk stone on its frill, burden in their slow feet, they weeping, she, *go on home,* in futility. There were dry-eyed cirri tracing the blue air that day. Pilate was that river I ran from leaving that woman, my mother, standing over its brutal green meaning and it was over by now and had become so ordinary as if not to see it any more, that constant veil over the eyes, the blood-stained blind of race and sex.

Leaving this standing, heart and eyes fixed to a
skyscraper and a concrete eternity not knowing then
only running away from something that breaks the
heart open and nowhere to live. Five hundred dollars
and a passport full of sand and winking water, is how
I reach here, a girl's face shimmering from a little
photograph, her hair between hot comb and afro, feet
posing in high heel shoes, never to pass her eyes on
the red-green threads of a hummingbird's twitching
back, the blood warm quickened water colours of a
sea bed, not the rain forest tangled in smoke-wet,
well there it was. I did read a book once about a
prairie in Alberta since my waving canefield wasn't
enough, too much cutlass and too much cut foot, but
romance only happen in romance novel, the concrete
building just overpower me, block my eyesight and
send the sky back, back where it more redolent.

Is steady trembling I trembling when they ask me my
name and say I too black for it. Is steady hurt I feeling
when old talk bleed, the sea don't have branch you
know darling. Nothing is a joke no more and I right
there with them, running for the train until I get to find
out my big sister just like to run and nobody wouldn't
vex if you miss the train, calling Spadina *Spadeena*
until I listen good for what white people call it, saying I
coming just to holiday to the immigration officer when
me and the son-of-a-bitch know I have labourer mark
all over my face. It don't have nothing call beauty
here but this is a place, a gasp of water from a
hundred lakes, fierce bright windows screaming with
goods, a constant drizzle of brown brick cutting
dolorous prisons into every green uprising of bush.
No wilderness self, is shards, shards, shards,
shards of raw glass, a debris of people you pick your way
through returning to your worse self, you the thin
mixture of just come and don't exist.

I walk Bathurst Street until it come like home
Pearl was near Dupont, upstairs a store one
christmas where we pretend as if nothing change we,
make rum punch and sing, with bottle and spoon,
song we weself never even sing but only hear when
we was children. Pearl, squeezing her big Point
Fortin self along the narrow hall singing *Drink a rum
and a ...* Pearl, working nights, cleaning, Pearl beating
books at her age, Pearl dying back home in a car
crash twenty years after everything was squeezed in,
a trip to Europe, a condominium, a man she suckled
like a baby. Pearl coaxing this living room with a
voice half lie and half memory, a voice no room
nowhere could believe was sincere. Pearl hoping this
room would catch fire above this frozen street. Our
singing parched, drying in the silence after the
chicken and ham and sweet bread effort to taste like
home, the slim red earnest sound of long ago with the
blinds drawn and the finally snow for christmas and
the mood that rum in a cold place takes. Well, even
our nostalgia was a lie, skittish as the truth these
bundle of years.

But wait, this must come out then. A hidden verb
takes inventory of those small years like a person
waiting at a corner, counting and growing thin
through life as cloth and as water, hush ... Look I
hated something, policemen, bankers, slavetraders,
shhh ... still do and even more these days. This city,
mourning the smell of flowers and dirt, cannot tell
me what to say even if it chokes me. Not a single
word drops from my lips for twenty years about living
here. Dumbfounded I walk as if these sidewalks are a
place I'm visiting. Like a holy ghost, I package the
smell of zinnias and lady of the night, I horde the taste
of star apples and granadilla. I return to that once
grammar struck in disbelief. Twenty years. Ignoring
my own money thrown on the counter, the race
conscious landlords and their jim crow flats, oh yes!
here! the work nobody else wants to do ... it's good
work I'm not complaining! but they make it taste bad,
bitter like peas. You can't smile here, is a sin, you
can't play music, it too loud. There was a time I could
tell if rain was coming, it used to make me sad the
yearly fasting of trees here, I felt some pity for the
ground turned hot and cold. All that time taken up
with circling this city in a fever. I remember then, and
it's hard to remember waiting so long to live ... anyway
it's fiction what I remember, only mornings took a long
time to come, I became more secretive, language
seemed to split in two, one branch fell silent, the other
argued hotly for going home.

This is the part that is always difficult, the walk each
night across the dark school yard, biting my tongue
on new english, reading biology, stumbling over
unworded white faces. But I am only here for a
moment. The new stink of wet wool, driving my legs
across snow, ice, counting the winters that I do not
skid and fall on, a job sorting cards, the smell of an
office full of hatred each morning, no simple hatred,
not for me only, but for the hated fact of an office, an
elevator stuffed with the anger of elevator at 8 a.m.
and 5 p.m., my voice on the telephone after nine
months of office and elevator saying, I have to spend
time on my dancing. Yes, I'm a dancer, it's my new
career. Alone in the room after the phone crying at
the weakness in my stomach. Dancer. This romance
begins in a conversation off the top of my head, the
kitchen at Grace Hospital is where it ends. Then the
post office, here is escape at least from femininity,
but not from the envy of colony, education, the list of
insults is for this, better than, brighter than, richer
than, beginning with this slender walk against the
mountainous school. Each night, the black crowd of
us parts in the cold darkness, smiling.

The truth is, well, truth is not important at one end of a hemisphere where a bird dives close to you in an ocean for a mouth full of fish, an ocean you come to swim in every two years, you, a slave to your leaping retina, capture the look of it. It is like saying you are dead. This place so full of your absence, this place you come to swim like habit, to taste like habit, this place where you are a woman and your breasts need armour to walk. Here. Nerve endings of steady light pinpoint all. That little light trembling the water again, that grey blue night pearl of the sea, the swirl of the earth that dash water back and always forth, that always fear of a woman watching the world from an evening beach with her sister, the courage between them to drink a beer and assume their presence against the coralline chuckle of male voices. In another place, not here, a woman might ... Our nostalgia was a lie and the passage on that six hour flight to ourselves is wide and like another world, and then another one inside and is so separate and fast to the skin but voiceless, never born, or born and stilled ... hush.

In another place, not here, a woman might touch
something between beauty and nowhere, back there
and here, might pass hand over hand her own
trembling life, but I have tried to imagine a sea not
bleeding, a girl's glance full as a verse, a woman
growing old and never crying to a radio hissing of a
black boy's murder. I have tried to keep my throat
gurgling like a bird's. I have listened to the hard
gossip of race that inhabits this road. Even in this I
have tried to hum mud and feathers and sit peacefully
in this foliage of bones and rain. I have chewed a few
votive leaves here, their taste already disenchanting
my mothers. I have tried to write this thing calmly
even as its lines burn to a close. I have come to know
something simple. Each sentence realised or
dreamed jumps like a pulse with history and takes a
side. What I say in any language is told in faultless
knowledge of skin, in drunkenness and weeping,
told as a woman without matches and tinder, not in
words and in words and in words learned by heart,
told in secret and not in secret, and listen, does not
burn out or waste and is plenty and pitiless and loves.

CHRISTOPHER DEWDNEY

THE CENOZOIC ASYLUM

As I paused to look I saw that the lower end which had been sweeping the ground was beginning to rise. I knew what that meant, so I kept my position. I knew that I was comparatively safe and I knew that if the tornado dipped again I could drop down and close the door before any harm could be done.

Steadily the tornado came on, the end gradually rising above the ground. I could have stood there only a few seconds but so impressed was I with what was going on that it seemed like a long time. At last the great shaggy end of the funnel hung directly overhead. Everything was as still as death. There was a strong gassy odour and it seemed that I could not breathe. There was a screaming, hissing sound coming directly from the end of the funnel. I looked up and to my astonishment I saw right up into the heart of the tornado. There was a circular opening in the centre of the funnel, about 50 or 100 feet in diameter, and extending straight upward for a distance of at least one half mile, as best I could judge under the circumstances. The walls of this opening were of rotating clouds and the whole was made brilliantly visible by constant flashes of lightning which zigzagged from side to side. Had it not been for the lightning I could not have seen the opening, not any distance up into it anyway.

Around the lower rim of the great vortex small tornadoes were constantly forming and breaking away. These looked like tails as they writhed their way around the end of the funnel. It was these that made the hissing noise. I noticed that the direction of rotation of the great whirl was anticlockwise, but the small twisters rotated both ways – some one way and some another.

The opening was entirely hollow except for something I could not exactly make out, but I supposed it was a detached wind cloud.

WILL KELLER, a Kansas farmer,
June 22, 1928

Grid Erectile

Because of its erotic & cool underparts & the sunset emblazoned on its
  membranous back. Its electric litheness.
Because it is a living precipitate of twilight.
Because it is large & soft with external gills.
Because it is tropical and changes colours.
Because the pattern on its back is a thin point.
Because they are so numerous and docile.
Because it whispers through foliage. An animate mobile tendril of
  chlorophyll.
Because it is like an adder, spawning mythology.
Because it is beautiful like a sleek girl with a choker.
For the milk sliding couples beaded with honey.
Because it is large & primitive & therefore closer to the dinosaurs.
Because they are the only lizards we have.
Because they fly around mercury vapour lamps at night & alight on
  suburban screens with their exotic & large bodies.
Because of their silent glittering black flight.
Because of a summer evening in 1954. It opened its wings & I received
  its revelation.
Because of summer nights behind the mosque.
Because it signals the height of summer.
Because of its mathematical precision at the infinite disposal of curiosity.
  Because its markings are the summation of military heraldry, the olive
  green of the English military.
Because it is a tropical species here in Southwestern Ontario.
Because they are nocturnal, tropical thin points of extreme beauty.
  Sculptural perfection in living and dense wood.
Because their chrysalis resembles a vase. Their humming flight & the
  insoluble intricacy of their June camouflage.
Because of the size & gothic modelling of their pincers, their chestnut
  brown elytra.
Because it is so tiny. (Weighs as much as a dime.)
Because it is pale underneath. Tawny above.
Because it is the eyes of night.
Because it is even larger, like a fox bat.

Because it is our largest and only cat.

Because they are capricious night gliders.

Because it is a predator.

Because of its inky fur. Tunnels twisting around roots.

Because it is a southern species migrating northwards. Evidence for an inter-glacial warming trend.

Because of their glowing eyes in the driveway at night. Their rasping marsupial cries.

Because of the caves.

Because of its unearthly face.

Because it is all of night.

Because it is a falcon.

Because it is sub-tropical.

Because it is a stilted & accurate blue mist.

Because it is the north, unwarranted in an ox-bow pond.

Because it is a tropical species slowly migrating north, starting at Point Pelee.

Because it is a sub-tropical iridescent metal.

Because it is the arctic migrating at the centre of blizzards.

Because they are astonishing aerialists.

Because the vacuum of space is so near.

Because of a dream.

Because they draw out the soul.

Anticipation. Electric gradients. The irresistible approach of the arc hammer. Excitation in the ion shadows.

Because they come after you & seem to float in dreams, the bend sinister.

Because of the storm.

Because of an erotic insularity in the moist almost tropical wind.

Because they illuminate everything in a grey powdery light and turn the outside into a surreal theatre of marvellous intent. The warmth allows the spectators to remove their clothes.

Lunacy & a saturnalian trance of corporeal clarity.

Because they are tropical.

Because they are both out of place & welcome.

Because they witnessed extinct races of fabulous creatures.

Because it is carnivorous & wet.

Because it is a carnivorous morning jewel in the sphagnum.

Because they are full lips & vulvas & are all of summer.

Because they are a tropical species here in Southwestern Ontario.

Because it has huge leaves and is tropical with cerise jurassic fruit.

Because it is fragrant & tropical.

Because its fruits are pungent.

Because the flowers are huge. Night glowing & perfumed.

Because of the pools.

Because their smooth mahogany pebbles are enclosed in vegetable geodes.

Because of fovea centralis.

Because they flowered all of beneath into above and translated it perfectly.

Because it is a living fossil.

Because of the colour & smoothness of its bark, the silence & level loam floor of the beech forest.

Because of the fragrance of its gum.

Because of the wooden petals of their flowers.

Because of the waterfalls & the morning glen.

Because it is the memory capital of Canada.

Because I perceived an order there.

Because the concretions are there.

Because of mid-summer nights, memory steeped in fireflies.

Because it overlooks Lake Huron.

Because the cedar pools are nearby.

For it was once submerged.

Because it is a huge invisible river.

Because of the collections in grey powdery light of Toronto winter afternoons spent in the devonian era.

Because it is semi-tropical & on the same latitude as California.

Because it is a cathedral of limestone.

Because it is awesome.

Because chronology was commenced there.

Because of the black river formation. Last hold-out of the White Elm.

Because of the beech forest & what came after.

Because I got to know Lake Erie & glacial clay there.

Because I grew up beside them & they taught me everything I know.

Because it is a huge & silent underwater predator.
Because it is huge and primitive.
Because it cruises, hovering, long snouted crocodilian.
Because it is primitive.

WOODEN ALVEOLI erect & fragile in the rarefied air of October, leaves frosted glass rock chapel orange & red. The sky no longer enclosing us. The filters removed there are desperate dreams in this woodlot. The airplane's engine blossoming into clarity & not enclosed. Eels are pulled from the canal. Even the planets are motile, hoary with diamonds above the chiming sunset. She swims alone & naked in a clear October lake. A white building stands free & O the spirits look dimly out from there.

A light impossibly orange as June evenings are a pastel rainbow of dreams & mercury vapour lamps, giant mantids, just coming on over the shopping plaza. The violet & pink light setting tanned skin aglow & each muscle a new surrender. The quiet village streets technologized in the telephoto insignia, lush nightfall still after a summer shower. The expectant interglacial period gardens, their scale-speed hierarchies squandered in the night. Stars arbitrate the carnivorous writhing of cycads.

The pool magnifies its own refractive distortion. Spring-fed the precise internal branches of underwater plants weave gently over the pale turquoise clay. Milky green glass, night conscious of itself, is secreted in large fragments at the base of the cedars surrounding the pool. A small palisade has been constructed for our convenience.

The elevator at Niagara opens to gardens on both levels. The floral dais reified in the fossil-fuel atmosphere. Q.E.W. into powdery acknowledgment of the planets' ascension. The red image of the setting sun, opalized through cirrus haze, reflected necessarily from the car windows. Charmed particles of dusk around the mercury vapour lamps. Themselves feeding voraciously on the scuttling metal flashing beneath them.

Vector obsolescent the radio bicycle futurizes its immediate tunnel. Summer glen of green grass & tall cedar & spruce. The spider's web beaded with morning dew. An abacus in the gravitational field of the moon.

The envelope of consciousness, as we are to the generator, surrounded by an aureole of dissolving nucleotides. Which freezes like winter the majesty of a summer night sky. Glade solstice of the internal summer, a tender explosion in the last enclave annihilate. Her nipples stiffen, flakes of come peel off like cellophane. Her delicate white legs unfoalding.

EACH FIGMENT profound the music is blown glass & cruelty turning on some spit. Fired by the vast machinery of the stars and their mysterious burning. Each house encloses a novel dusk, turning off all the lights. Windows opening on both sides to giant trees, still as dew in the summer night. Water nymphs enclose themselves in warm limestone streams. Fireflies pinpoint cool luminous ideas in the neural foliage of dreams.

Genital clusters. Leaf grotto.

A translucent saturn, large as the moon, ascends behind the vacant observatory. In starlit fields unearthly children recite an embrace in whose absence?

The underwater paradigm of your eternal existence in sunlit brook chambers. Bend sinister freed the broken consort. And we built a temple in the warm night air. The giant hollyhock flower looming paraboloid in the visual scan of the hover-fly. With cells shining gold rings & thin amulets around the corporeal swarm. The occasional giant thrusting through the canopy, their branches bending in the rainless wind of a nocturnal heat storm. The body is assembled around the perceptions. Tiny iridescent bees. The wind soft thunder in our ears. Reagent command the word transcribed. Tactile revelation of the optical sector, only the blue megahertz evening stars ascending over the garden wall. The anvil tops of cumulonimbus graze the stratosphere, moonlight high over the storm. This is witnessed by a small passenger airliner lost in the thirties. Sucrose in the infinite capillary network of the horse chestnut. The sub-canopies dangle in ever rising cascades of green. The levels consistent through which the forest sylph winds, light as to have been a rumour written in smoke.

Rivers of cool air flow in slow-motion cascades down the ravines. The heavy air sliding beneath trees sustained as bats inverting flicker darkly through desire. Fascination drove them into the shade. Aero-delta over the river a shock-wave of mist.

One pure burning heart.

The body is a slow fire, an infra-red jungle of thermal contours. The sun spiking triangular, fossil-jawed, the grain is blonde & shimmering. The evening sun on a lone crab apple tree halfway up the side of a bleached grassy hill, the blue windy sky.

IN AUGUST there is a second spring, bracken fiddleheads emerge in the north, magnolias bloom along the edge of limestone chasms. Wasp nests begin to bend the boughs suspend a newsprint vortex. The yellow jackets are attracted to meat, sweat and the odour of hot metal. Nighthawks stop calling in the early part of September. Between this time and the time they leave, some twenty days, is the silent summer. Carnivals spawn as August hardens into the lush & fecund empire of September. Leaves yellow & drop singly as in a rainforest drought. Heat showers drive the wasps from rotting peaches. Noctuids, mantises, cicadas & dragonflies as the insect population reaches its climax. Small predatory night breezes rustle through the undergrowth. Striped snails slumber beneath the leaves. Sweating bannisters. September is August enthroned. September is August parentheticized.

A very neural humour, as if your name, determined telepathically, had been mistakenly pronounced in Chinese. Wired the first angelic rays spiking horizontal above our heads. Pealing off the line of evening in fluted stars. Tide rising eventide to White Sands.

In a dream there is a basement.

Auto-erotic signals shimmer through the further reaches of the organism. Buds emerge red into green. Panther arrests the paw-paw triumphant, July haze down the lane, hanging gardens & old wood in the garage. Giant scarabaeidae larvae, white & translucent blue stuffed saran jewels in the hollow oak's loam. The coprolitic chrysalis cases, grub-loam geodes & the sculpted obsidian deities within. Pelidnota & Osmoderma. Brasilia, harlequin nocturne. Giant flickering scarabs orbit the night lights of a factory in Manaus. All the machinery stands poised & glistening. The nighthawks return, a contracting pupil of magic around the light-field of the city. They are surveillance.

Metaphorical objects & models are precipitated by synesthesia into mimics of the very adjuncts to reality out of which human perception arranges itself.

Burning the river dry the nights of forest celebrations & softly glowing veins of opal fluorescing in the depths clairvoyant of limestone gorges.

THE RAIN of sensorium is erosion is the absolute event horizon exposing memory. High relief from the rock matrix. Form withstanding erosion. Fovea Centralis now moving through the words. A lax penis spewing sperm into a somnambulistic & female constellation. Our actions tiny eddies & whirlpools on the surface of a mirror-still planetary ocean. Ripples indicating the stirrings of chinese dragons deep within.

Perihelion of the cicada through the brassy July sky, schemata of blue pepsis vectors. An orange patch of sun in the evening forest. Symphonies in the distant night traffic. Sand flats beside the river under budding thickets of staghorn sumac, high-water nests in their boughs. Feeding hairline crack, a barn-storm translated into the propagation-lee of the glass machinery. Extension drift on the Tethys. The sound of distant waves. Hissing rain tires on the evening bridge. Fierce array of the spring foliage. Ourselves also. Strange progeny of a billion years of solar irradiation. All details threshold the effect delight.

Only the blue megahertz evening stars ascending over the garden wall. Night unfolds like no other in her slickensided vagina. Juice flowing sustained by her witnessing. Slate limousines hissing rubber quietly offering cobblestones to the curb. The eventide rising high-rise moon to White Sands. Streamline yourself into the truth. Interference text. The nighthawks emerge from their hangars. The sun renewed within itself decreed our prodigious evolution. The grim satisfaction it gives you to watch your own face decay under the withering gaze you yourself have spawned in her. For that which is most completely out of control most clearly reveals the workings of the unseen machinations.

It is a warm grey day in August. A powdery luminescence oscillates within the patches of night beneath the trees. Nocturnal pools characterized by crickets & day foraging bats. A wind stirs the fissures of the canopy. What is still is expectant. Bat's dusky membranes envelop the writhing coils of a small snake, their standoff illuminated by the pink August dawn. A distant blue jay's call sounds the interceding forest. An albino fox in the cedar verge. Waves on Lake Huron in your sleep they are waves within breathing. The beach intersects distant momentums. Surges linger in a phantasmic waveform. Embro Foldens her children the lake claims by dreaming lay waste the armoured spinal cord. A delirious rush of invertebrate orgasms in the implacable recall of the ocean. I do not consider the waves empty in your sense(s). Free-fall under the swells a pulsing spinal thrill. Diving to the source of neural conductivity. Ammonites a copper mist gleaming dully through the shallow water. Peripheral glimpse of trilobites scuttling into murky water at the edge of the Ausable. Hungry Hollow Hills, memory vapour. Her lissome arms & legs trailing in the tepid summer water as the small boat rounds the bend into the canyon.

Deafening cicadas.

Fierce array of the summer foliage.

Re-group at the air-lock. Her spine ends in four extra vertebrae, prehensile as a finger she shoves it up your ass as you come. Her parents obviously intrigued by the sexual options in the genetic engineering catalogue. She has slight webs between her fingers. The limestone heaves up & dissolves in an awesome rumbling giving up all the time trapped in its layers. Legions of extinct creatures crawl up through the rubble, transparent with age. The planets converge & hover just beyond the atmosphere in the evening sky, barely opaque in the haze. The electromagnetic fields generate huge scarab beetles. Iridescent elytra & fabulous horns. Cascade of night & night wind coming in the living-room window drugged & cool. Full moon. Only the brightest stars glowing in the soft blue summer night. I have learned to love the noctuids.

Cumulonimbus clouds towering with their bases just below the horizon. Pink in the gasoline haze & slanting rays of the setting sun. Billowing like the convoluted foreheads of brooding foetuses, their water-brains filled with grotesque electric thought impulses & thunder. Their silence raining onto the land.

A CONSENUAL DOMAIN in the unrelenting hunger of her mouths, glistening lacunae in a tactile confluence of mass. Merely her proximity. The granular phrasing of her ass. Faint blue lace-work of veins beneath the lactose silk of her breasts. Multi-foliate her orgasms an interlocking network of pure sensual detail rippling through the surrounding forest. Saturnidae moths in vibrating clusters, wings still unfolding, still damp with emergence. Electric gradients in the anticipation zone of her touching. Sunset glittering in the windows of the planetarium.

Full summer moon rising obliquely over the pitcher plants and miniature sphagnum landscapes. Vigilance. Panavistic crystal night-vision of the silver lynx, silhouetted for an instant against the ocellus of the summer moon. Hypnotic cameo resumed without juncture. Stars dripping from the points of mulluscoid teats.

There can be no highlights if there is no point of view. No reflections, no rainbows. The virtual image is subject dependent.

Slickensided fluting of the terminator line, evening stars pealing off like no other the velvet theatre curtains undulating slowly in the night wind, their lower folds wet with pond water. Distant red glow of smelters and factories to the north. Hydrogen pumps. Autoclave the glacial clay bluffs & narrow pebble beach of Tyrconnell. A mathematical plain in critical grey light the unlikely appearance of Cenozoic bi-valves. Runaway crouches in the amphibious June musk of Byron Bog. Heat-weave sun vibrato through the moist forest floor, naked feet on spongy humus, exotic insects splashing sudden erratic trajectories over the path. Linnaeus a certain key.

Blue fluid support of summer sky eggshell into evening explorations of sexual forests hot naked waists in the cool night air an intangible barrier realizing the planet's dream. Green leaf-haze of April branches. Image without recognition equal to total configuration surrounding her. The forest is alive with itself, vegetable leather leaves of the rhododendron. Behind manifestation is manifestation. Slim curve of her waist generated through the plane of symmetry. Her pelvis vaulted like angel's wings just barely surfacing in the smooth tautology of her hips. Her come spangled down. Drops of semen deliquescing in the naked morning spectra. Her nipples glazed & wrinkled. Within the forest a vapour resounds.

Nomenclature of rivulets, the dense and kinematic vegetation of the ravine incalculable. Coal-swamp dusk in advance of the terminator line. Mute & recoiled September is a nation of secret pacts. Summerhill, bleached grass with a lone hawthorn tree halfway against the late afternoon polaroid receding blue sky. Maple leaves unfolding jazz-wrist into pale bat wings. Giant hairy fiddleheads of the tree fern. Distant nighthawks beckoning from the bluff of the line storm. Norse gold forged in orgasms & sun her face vigilant in the first humid cobalt June storm wind. Summer copper dusted pale green. She runs the palm of her right hand lightly over her left breast, her nipples erect ozone the wind soft thunder in our ears.

There is no season uncorrupt of another. Distant tropical storm at night in our breathing. In the heart of fall there is a summer glen. Evening cicadas. Heat storm. White violet flickering sudden silhouettes the frozen forest staggered omni-directional. Sassafras grove in the ravine incalculable. Lobed canopy occasionally divulging the pale blue eggshell evening, silver down underneath. Raccoons awakening on oak branches, heat-wave somnolence their masked regard. Wild grape vines. Dark coils draped in the lower branches.

She hands & knees hung belly her breasts I slowly push my cock into the spreading liquid fire. Constant gushing thrill the night permeated. Eyes, ears, mouth, nostrils, genitals, hands & feet. A night unmoved by the crickets until dawn. Red haven. Free stone. Midnight in the hyper-personal theatre of an August moon. Its reflection in the lake an electric mirage loomed a dazzling monotonous dream light. The water quick molecular sand.

Ascend & merge.

SUNNY HARPSICHORD forest morning blending imperceptibly into afternoon. Night the Cenozoic asylum. All mammals quickened in the autumn, their organisms burning more fiercely. Distant FM Satie on deserted terraces. The glass machinery intact as if an overlay filled equally with allusion. The music stripped pure of association. A heart burning bittersweet the dreams surrounding it. As if paradise renewed a tangible & immaculate perception. The fall from grace is the remove itself. Caught in the first fine figments of ice on the October pond. An ice palace deep in the autumn forest, skating down cool summer department corridors of green & red. Ancient summer snakes, Don & Humber wild fingers deep into the city. Silver mist audio-fog, an electronic grey day over Lake Huron. Anticipation slicked water lapping Devon beaches. Glistening conglomerate of the pebble incline. Eleuthera blue. Weird music of the stars, raining down silently upon all of this.

We have always made love this way, down through all the ages. Archaeopteryx rising glittering to the surface of the lithographic stone. Distant amphetamine lovemaking. A white apartment building in the blue summer night. The moon. A woman waiting up there. Empty sunlight building. End of the sparkling fiord. A stonehouse chiaroscuro of yellow leaves the sun torn polaroid blue & white Lawren Harris. Mysterious ariels their red lights glowing in the coastal twilight. Mood beacons of inexplicable childhood memories. The orchestra suddenly quiet.

The summers that were and the summers that never were.

Words from silence hatched.

                              & its surface glistening with
                              paraboloids.

The night sand cool at the surface & warm beneath. Pink, blue & orange ultra-violet dimly through the tree ferns. The scenery strobes slightly under the hot overcast swamp vision. Limestone outcrops. Dew drunk cecropia moths aimlessly copulating with flowers, twigs, hypothermic dragonflies & fingers. Perfect curve of muscular sine flesh burning pink & blue & orange cool sand crumbling like granular cork over her budding cellular nipples. Unnatural grace of her moving. Thick spurting unrestrained into her urgent & delicate choreography. Silk & gold. Leaves sliding long taut abdominal trails behind the skin palace cool devon cream. Darkly traced in a silence our eyes do not seam.

THERE IS a second order of darkness rarely witnessed. Brick walls radiating tangible heat at midnight. Tiny black rivulets of tar congealed in diminutive lava flows. Lithographic stone the miniature jungle of a summer lawn. Satie distant fingers on vacant FM patios at night. Calibrations returning from a starry pasture.

Her tendrils alarming hyperbolas in the dim atmospheric envelope. Embryology. Insect resumé presumed the manifest diode resplendent. Toroidal gravity nets. Wind a cheering shield of leaves, flickering shadows on the pale beech cinematic beneath the canopy. Buttressed against the observer's opaque logos this island arraigned through the visual scan of a hover fly. The expressway burnt amber shimmering with thermal inversion puddles. Staggered grace the thin metal of rain on the pond's surface.

The hum of huge electric engines and factories low in the distance. Clouds of dust and cool forest the monotone is sustained by the whistling hordes of vacuum eyed marsupials filing quickly into the city. The trees, straining in terror, almost achieve visible movement. The impossible children's valleys crumble through backyards & living-rooms. Lips are drawn over the teeth in crawling fear of the words being formed.

The angel of revelation descends down the line of vision. When the eyes fix the annunciation begins. A distant star over the attenuated autumn foliage. Herald of the anti-dawn. Delta of venus fore-winged with vernal espionage & silver. The declension a focal sphere contracting around fovea centralis, the perfect fossil of an unknown species that will never be found. The lions & unicorns we wish to speak through.

LOUIS DUDEK

AT LAC EN COEUR

1

What kind of honey does a bee get from a thistle?
A purple bomb, toxic
                with spears of language.

Hating pretentiousness,
                or the vanity of writing poems,
I sit for hours without a word.

The hidden bios, cosmos, works with his emotions
shaping things into multiform shapes of desire.

He never says a word
                nor even (perhaps) thinks a thought
but fits the liver under the beating heart
as the artist places his cove and tree,
                feeling his way
                to the complex unities.

We cross-section this work of love
                when we think or talk.

2

Nothing is eternal. Not even the trees
though I gather that some are longer-lived than a man.

A whirling flashlight
                    makes a permanent wheel.
Moving lights. We are a web.

Unity, out of motion and diversity,
                    as real as atoms.

The blue sky turning pale green at the horizon,
only one streak of cloud
                    beyond the birch leaves overhead.

The trees, cedar, some maple, and tattered pine,
below them the fern and smaller brush,

dead leaves, brown earth, rock
(a canoe on the still water makes a slapping sound)

And I sit, the ache in my bones receding,
                    a thought breathing cold air –

shaping a world already made
                    to a form that I require.

3

Since all things contemplate themselves
a mouse in a ditch
                    observes itself,

in silence, slips underground
in solitude eats, twitches, curls and sleeps ...

Does no one approve? No one care?
How can he exist —
                    alone?

A mouse goes without fear, alone, as if
            with love's eye upon it.

4

Cottages like Chinese lanterns
               shine in the soft dark
I breathe the moist night, by the lakeside

Fishes peer at our intrepid lights,
                    ephemeral man-blown stars
in their familiar trees

The road is lit by a small lamp
waving with my body's swing,
             rocked at the pelvis, to and fro,

as I pass, leaving the great
              shadows behind
and the green domes in the night.

5

Some men murder fishes, others kill quail
all for sport. The trees fall
like great sick animals, eaten by the saprophytes in their sides.

We have no time, to hate or mourn.
Love the arrowy fern, mean moss, and furry bee
enough to forgive all

fools out of despair
that, dying, cover fear
with laughter, guns, or game on a hook.

6

Alone in the forest
I hear the wind overhead,
        see the lake through the trees.

Several monsters are allayed.
I sit on a high rock, alone,
listening to the wind, looking through the pines.

In front of me a fir
sends up a central stalk
        with four pedicles around it

(only by keeping apart from the others
                        can it assert that form)

curving from the four corners, a cup, kylix
                        (a word, language),
below this the various branches

end in four-pronged stems,
        one, the longest, bearing the end-bud,
others minors, keeping proportion.

The whole thing somewhat isolated
                from the smothering multitude –
a complete architecture of organic meaning.

Perfect to live, alone, lonely,
aspiring and self-fulfilled, growing, in a cleft,
                on this high rock,
with only the wind and sky to see and hear.

7

But a flower torn off from the stem does not know
what a tragedy has occurred,
                              a waterlily

opens and closes with the day
                              on our table
as though it were a vase in a lake.

Rootless flowers!
whose individuation is yet a part of their form ...

To live, become immune
            to every bleeding cosmic wound.

8

The shapes, I think them
        as of waves coming in
        lapping the curve of the shore,
                and wind carving clouds,
may be or not be as I perceive

but the fruit of the maple, pine cone,
seed of the cedar (proving Goethe's principle,
        every compartment
a form like the flattened branch and whole tree)

formed out of the flux, are there
atomic, mobile –
        unities that persist,
real as in a mind.

9

Who thinks the living universe?
I think it but in part.
Fragments exist
            like those infinitesimal separate stars
I saw, lying on my back on the cushions
last night before the storm:

their union, as powers
            but as wheels on the one axle,
and as form –
      a drawing by a master hand.

We have united some few pigments
            (all that is in museums)
but the greater part, all life, was there
                        united when we came –
and grows, a copious language of forms.

Who thinks them? …
            Their being is a thought.

My thought, a part of being – is a tree
of many thoughts, in which a yellow bird sits.

In the silence, sitting in the silence
I seem to hear the visible language speak

                                 a leaf

(a glimpse of paradise perhaps to be)

Here in hell, in purgatorio,
all things suffer this waiting, become
only then whatever they will be:
ecstasies of creation, flowers
               opening ecstatic lucent leaves.

Nothing else matters.
Nothing else speaks.

II

So beauty
it says, so quietly in the shadows
that a small bird
                on a red bomb
shrieks a symphonic whistle
just turning its head, without a sound from the throat.

Anywhere the eyebeam transects the world, a thorn
strikes with such sharpness to a thought.

Lac En Coeur

I had so far made it my concern
                    not to be aware
of writing a poem, thought of it
as irrelevant,
as in this case anyhow contrary
                    to my real concern,

that I wrote nothing
                    I did not first think
complete, as it stands.
Not a poem, but a meditation –
          they make themselves, are also natural forms,

kernels that come whole to the hand.

DIANA HARTOG

OASIS

Although we see Celestial bodies move
above the earth, the earth we Till and love

John Donne

Creation, 3:30 p.m., the Fifth Day

A lynx prowls past in the shade of the porch, her tufted ears pricked to the
silent jangling of her many bracelets,

followed by her mate, the two leaving pawprints like walking fists across the
sand as they climb the dune and
disappear into the tamarisk on their rounds
of the Animal Kingdom. *I must not yet be here.*

Oasis

The sound of each other, rustling,
the easy exchange through the air of insects and birds.

Noon, and to the south
mercury shimmers in the wind-tousled palms.

Near, they loom as mammoths, skirted with brown
down-drooping layers of years vulnerable to a
dropped match, a stray spark catching the imagination
where a trunk issues blackened and shorn.

In the hallowed clearing – palms towering in a shaggy ring –
recurs the wedding of Place and Time, attended by a sand-beetle
and mourned by the wind – which foresees with a rustle of taffeta
the early death of the bride.

       With evening,
what has died is the wind.

On the bluff, every creosote bush has gathered to a nucleus
its quail for the night: all one can safely know. The birds doze
in circles, facing out, ready to scatter in overlapping rings at
the slightest mention.

Drifting, the high moon keeps its distance, holds it close
as I would be held.
                Let me guess: in a pool
half-hidden by reeds floats another moon – gilded, tremulous
from the glide of a water-spider. Am I close?
Am I even warm?

The Seventh Day

In the shimmering heat every plant grows jealous
of its dime of shade, the coyotes slinking
backwards, all needs shrunken and
withdrawn into the brainstem

though at dawn, the sharp spine of a cactus will attract
a single drop of dew and roll the tear down into the eye.

Forty days, we are told, and forty nights, Christ
consumed only his hunger,
and poured cool thirst over his shoulders
as he sat, studying the palm of the human hand.

A Thirst for Knowledge

I

Grain by grain, and gaining momentum with a shudder of sand down its flank, the white dune inches south, wormy with lizards. From the cool, loose interior the reptiles slither fringe-toed to the surface and air. Here they arch their necks, flood with warmth, and pursue the single blank thought of their species, the two beads of mercury unblinking. The creature holds still, perfectly still

as I climb, and stoop
for the wizened leather glove: petite, the two eyes
unbuttoned at the wrist.

II

In the sky floats the white moon, thin as a wafer of Communion melting on the tongue; shrapnel lured from afar, from some previous disaster. Or perhaps a moon of our own rib, as I would hazard, one tethered and swung in an arc from the mind's Third Eye; a moon along the lines of a groove worn in the blue irreducible, a mote followed by the longing of oceans and the surface, disturbed, of every single cup of tea.

But I could be wrong.

Chimney Ranch

Under a vast black sky sparkling with tomorrow's ashes,
tonight's stars, lies a grave bowered by tamarisk.

"Build the chimney first," he is known to have said, kneeling
to lay twigs upon crumpled news of the quick.

I find him sleeping on the roof, with an arm
      thrown over his face
to ward off the Pleiades – those black-skirted Sisters
who in his youth fed him from a trine of spoons
the taste of Brass, of Lead, and of
mercury's skittish Absence: Choose, they insisted, Choose!

Alone, and scanning overhead the firing neurons, the expanding
limits of the brain, I decide there is time, plenty of
time left,
        as now I lay me down,
                to refuse.

Nightclass

The Mad Professor shouts, taps the blackboard with a stick
and paces to explain the great mating and uncoupling
of the planets: the retrograde dance, the southern reeling
of those ideas known as stars.

He cranks the system by hand
and the painted tin globes of Mercury & Venus & Mars –
    stiff-armed on wires –
revolve by jerks around a sun with the rind of a grapefruit,
the sundry moons (some as tiny as peas) racing dizzily

As the homeless of an L.A. alley lie stretched full-length
on broken sofas in the street: smoking, gazing up through a blur
of smog, at the flickering light of past mistakes
they can now pinpoint.

The Moon and Firestone

Let's take a look at the moon as a beautiful woman – half-angry,
half-full. Ringed with industry's sanguine fumes she rises
above the Hollywood Freeway, Friday midnight, clots of traffic
moving sluggishly if at all, the cars' occupants
audience to this B-Grade movie, an old one with Bette Davis
   ascending the staircase in a close-up; the atmosphere
exaggerating every pore of a landscape cratered with hurled rocks,

while privately, beneath the overpass, the heavy *thud* of
   someone's heart
is let drop to the sidewalk in a brown paper bag.

Though the city has limits – a stutter of lights, virgin
culs-de-sacs, half-acre lots yet to be sold where a cloverleaf
juts into unfinished space; the cured concrete dangles steel
reinforcement above a man hurrying home at dawn, clutching
a new Sunbeam toaster, the cut on his hand bleeding

as fields of strawberries and the bent knuckled spines
of migrants in flowered shirts flash by,
harvested in turn by desert, where armies of windmills
flail the Santa Ana winds
and waving billboard palms solicit at every Exit
as the highway eases from pavement to gravel to dirt, to a trail
freshed by coyotes trotting north to the next oasis, in search of
fallen dates in this Garden.

Settling for Palm Springs
the white morning moon
allows the mundane purchase of four steel-belted radials
to eclipse her briefly – their mounting and balancing –
as she drifts, pale and ethereal, above the dealership;
a moon snubbed with cigarette butts; smudged; erased;
a sphere rounded-off to the last digit of the national debt,

yet still she comes around, a satellite lured into orbit
around our hardened metallic core, as if we were interesting
and might change;
a moon drawn, presumably, by what she sees as her own
   strewn phrases
in the tire dumps, acres of black rinds

Glass

With a lurch, an earthquake visits
and I grope for the switch – the gooseneck lamp
bent low, as if to drink from the glass of trembling water.

I see that sand has drifted in across the night,
which explains my dream, of a meteorite
hurtling through webbed glass
to land softly on my stomach: still smoking yet strangely cold
and the size of a scorched orange.

I smoothe the counterpane, inspect a tiny cigarette burn.
That worn bullet-hole in the window
will have to be stopped.

The Link Between Reader and Writer

Perhaps you're sitting up in bed, and have tilted
the light to the page so as not to disturb lying beside you
another person.

Or listening for the children's squeals from the
upstairs tub, you have gone to kneel
and with a towel blot their sturdy little bodies

— leaving this face down on the couch.

Outside in the random silence, the desert wind
is jangling against the flagpole
some metal thing.

Infra-Red

Black widows have crawled up under the skirts
of the Washingtonia *filifera,* and a sidewinder
wrapped its chill length around the warmth of a boulder
the way the mind, coiling around the brain,

drops off to sleep

among scorpions
burrowed into sand, and joins
their revolving ruby-movement: legions
in enamel and hammered gold, their stingers
arched, steering towards the furthest constellation.

Entry

The silence of the desert is too strong for the walls of the ranch house. The feeble bleats of the radio are overpowered at night by the presence of the high white dune to the west, by the whisper of the tamarisk over the empty, needle-lined pool; and even in here I can feel the stars through the ceiling, feel their glitter at the roof of my skull as each new spark of thought is snuffed in the darkness, in obeisance to those higher thoughts — of an Intelligence who thinks not in words but in Bears, Scorpions, Giants with fine diamond-edged swords; and sapphire-set Dippers, bent at the handle to scoop the mercury of memory, or whatever it is, off the top of our heads, that Gods drink.

Meridian

Water trickles into the ear: a stream snaking across the oasis.
Bees drone high in the medulla.
The yellowing cottonwood flowers with a sweet humming –
    consumed
when the swarm departs from the silenced limbs.

The silent Rudolph Valentino in *Son of the Sheik*
slipped his hand to the small of a starlet's back
and bent her to the kiss of all time

under this same moon: rising pale and pockmarked,
fragile against the blue,
for daylight
has again undone the moon

as we are all undone – lifting our arms, stretching.
We who have gravity to blame for how far
we fall, how soon
warm sand
slips through the narrow glass waist of the hour.

ROY KIYOOKA
PEAR TREE POMES

for Daphne & Kit

a tree becomes a nest the moment a great dreamer hides in it

Gaston Bachelard, "Nests"

credences of summer
now in midsummer come all fools slaughtered
and spring's infuriations over and a long way
to the first autumnal inhalations, young broods
are in the grass, the roses are heavy with a weight
of fragrance and the mind lays by its trouble.

now the mind lays by its trouble and considers.
the fidgets of summer come to this.
this is the last day of a certain year
beyond which there is nothing left of time.
it comes to this and the imagination's life.

Wallace Stevens

*

tall as a telephone pole and as old as the oldest house on
the block the pear tree lights up the whole sky above our alley
every spring and every fall it's a pear a day for every kid
who saunters down the alley – something round to bite into some-
thing ripe to splatter the nearest garage door with . i haven't
said a thing about its viridian summers or its charcoal winters
but as i sit here writing its virtues down on paper i can see
call it the "real" pear tree just outside the study window .
inside or outside of anywhich door or window there's at least
one pear tree unfolding the verities of all four seasons . intact
these words cling to each fragile blossom fruit bug and worm
the old pear tree exudes . if you listen closely you'll hear a
creaking branch with "me" clinging to it without a ping of remorse .

*

these bent rusted nails embedded in
the pear tree's trunk : these broken cleats speak
of a processional of school-children
barking their shins while skinning the pear tree
shimmying up into its leafy hideaway .

long after the very least pear on the last live twig
falls earthward "these" frost-bite words
shaped from a handful of dried stems will recall
their boisterous covenant. these bent words
embedded in my own trunk bespeak "other" plangencies

*

given the gift of its white blossoms the small yellow pears

to come "these" words want to spell out an old story of
how two lovers sat a round-of-seasons up in the forkt branches
of an old pear tree . like the birds the assorted birds percht
in its candelabrum-branches they would re-enact the magic
of each unfolding day up in their air-stream lair . given
the divers ways they were paired these words want to finger all
the silences that fell between them before each fell out
of its parasol of leaves in an unmitigated heap . given all
the time in the world only language never stops listening "to"
and "for" the other . only an "i" cries – havoc!

*

since you and i forsook the rites of marriage

intentionally without – facing up to the signals of mutual
disenchantment – we found ourselves side-stepping
each other's nakedness to fall asleep in a heap of mired feelings
til the early bird traffic on prior street summoned us
to another "good morning – did you sleep well" breakfast
on the run . there's a lady with a champagne voice on co-op radio
singin' the ol' after midnight blues and whoops! – there's
that ol' heart-ache again . what i want to know is how come you
with your bright gists and me with my pointed beard didn't
make the perfect match . how come we ended up playing
that ol' deaf and dumb game when it was as plain as this prose
that the pear tree's forkt branches foretold the truth .
since you left i've been taking a hot water bottle to bed
                    how about you with your tepid toes?

*

love the aurora of these late september nights

as i write this lovely suffusion of twilight colors down
it changes before my very surmise from rose into translucent amber .
by the time i get to the end of this petite colonnade of words
all the amber will be stained a deep violet and in a few moments ...
the pear tree's branches will have knit the night-sky around
themselves to catch a falling star . such as they are these words bear
a testimonial to all the weather we lived through together .
not even your leaving me for a woman will erase their intrepid
measure . love, the night-wind is winding up the spindle of another
dream .... where o where do you think it will spin us?

*

the pear tree's white blossoms tincture the night air

i remember turning away from the ah of that lovely stain
to place my head on your bare white shoulder . these words mime
the exactitude of your scent – even as they reach out to
cup the ah cool tingle of your pear-shaped breasts . last night's
sudden shower draws all the fragrances out of the grass .
i remember those other nights we stained with our unbidden tears
"tears" i later thought we had wrung from the riddled depth
of the pear tree's corrugated trunk . "into each life some rain
must fall ..." the ink spots wail on a/m radio and so it's off
to my small bed . any fleet whiff of another bod turns out to be
an unexpected wind-fall these dwindle-down rasp of days

*

given the gift of ground the pear tree shaded every summer

there will always be pears to look up at and pears to preserve
pears to bite into and toss and last but not least there'll
always be pears rotting into the ground to nourish the seed of a
small pome . – would you believe me if i said i want these
very words to turn into that pear you're biting into . believe me
biting into a ripe pear doesn't bear the same consequences as
biting into an apple . – just ask jack our cantonese neighbour.

*

since i wrote the night sky down i've been out for

a late night bowl of barbecue duck noodle soup at kam's garden
and since i got home i put the ol' blue mule band on and
yes – i've dreamt up this 6 a/m dawn just for you . i'm just
an ol' night bird ready to do the lindy hop with any ol'
hurdy-gurdy man or woman . "birds" who don't invest in the same
dawn tend to end up sharing a different nest . since you
left i've been keeping an early morning vigil .

*

if i had known the number of hours i would find myself mute

til the early morning wind off the tip of ballantyne pier gently
stirred every leaf and all of a sudden these words, these votaries of
incandescence, and all the awakened birds startle – the incipient
breath of a small pome. if i had known it would take 56 summers to
divine a plain-song i would, given another spin of the wheel chant
each new-born syllable aloft and watch it haunt the combustible air.
in this way the felicitous way of nouns and their attendant verbs –
a small pear made its compact with the sun to become utterly rotund.

"i breast an ancient syntax heaptup long before speech bore fruit …"
trilled an orange-crested pear tree bird before heading south

*

how to qualify a pear tree without pointing at the sky

i lean out of the study window to sniff the clear october night
there's one two three half-bitten pears hanging in mid-air

under skeletal branches a motley of bruised pears toll the end of
another summer, another fall, flagrant heat, heart and all

up in the air or down on the ground all creatures large and small
begin by biting the air these bitten pears bear the flesh of

*

who knows how long this small psalm to an old pear tree

and your preserved pears will sing into the so-called future.
on this the last friday in the month of august i am ravaged
by its gist of autumnal silences and everything it unconceals.
what i have been given to accomplish borrows something dark,
barely apprehensible from, it must be its original shadow .
planted in the rainforest of my image of a pacific nation the OM
of primal silences blew a pear tree the size of a dwarf's fist
into the forebodings of a sentence, which, believe it or not
flowered into, this bitten flesh, this beak of mirth

p/s caught a glimpse of jim the ace mechanic of our alley
biting into a ripe pear while over his head a bunch of starlings
and a robin you know have awful belly-aches.
                    ask a fallen pear about winter omens

*

since we stood on the back porch

wondering if the old pear tree would survive another winter ...
i've been sitting here where you used to sit writing its
diurnal virtues down on paper and every time i look up i can
see how it prevailed over our solicitudes by lofting yet
another plangent spring . with or without you i am clearly
intent upon sharing its equinoctial visions . riddled by
an awed phosphorescence : the old pear tree and i sit quietly
divining the lattices of a frugal winter light

*

in my book of sacral nomenclature

the pear tree bespeaks all the unimpeachable days
we savour'd under its green umbrella .
"pears" kisst into existence by the sun will nourish
compost and bury every lover . given
its seasonal epiphanies i would be a fool indeed if
i didn't turn inside its ring-of-seasons and
yes   sing my adamant self alive —

*

with his waterman fountain pen poised wallace stevens
meditated in front of a cut-glass bowl full of ripe pears
and the language he mediated mirrored their rotundness

i loved the whole smell of the morning world from the back porch
of 1008 third street east when i was a foothills child
i thought thinking of all the spells i had before i could spell

ask wallace stevens if an ode to an old pear tree sounds too
trifling to thrill the air of our well-being . ask mrs stevens
how come she had two green thumbs and eight brown fingernails

permit me to add that this bright fall morning enthralls each
pear left dangling from the old pear tree's boughs . ask "pear"
about the midnight arias sung in allah's scented groves . ...

*

a persian miniature for gerry and marlene

planted at the foot of the pear tree their endearments
curve towards each other on stamens of silence .
if you put your ear to its scarred trunk you'll overhear
the pizzicato of their least perturbation . nothing
you can dream up equals their exquisite forays
and scented rebuffs . if i had to do it up in a pear tree
again i would hide a tape deck in its lustrous leaves
to record the least tremble . given a tongue-tied
poet sitting in a pear tree with his beloved these words
are but a faint echo of their original betrothal .
planted at the foot of the pear tree their every endearment
composts love's etymologies . ask adam or eve

*

o
little
bird

chirp
pippa's
song

into
my blue
ear

*

love the subtle ways the weather occurs and reoccurs

in the bodies of men and women . love all the intricate ways
the world has of disappearing into their forebodings .
love there is no discourse left in the abode of language no
ecstasy or outrage left undesecrated no unconditional
"yes" – yet there's something unborn in me that wants to be
the "verb" of that longing my body feels when it feels
the actual touch of your breath . an appall'd lover bends his
ear to the pear tree's trunk to hear a lost rhetorick .

*

what lay under the midden the
mound of hair between her gated thighs
toucht his deepest presentiments .
permeable as a summer rain and twice as
penetrant she stroked the small
of his back til he curled up a child
in her ample lap and wept himself
to sleep . in the air-borne nest between
her speckled-breasts the pear tree
sang a psalm to the long-legged bride
and her goat-footed consort who
together with a gnomic child dwelled in
an all-weather pear tree house . it
sang them a salmon-haunted song
of all the lost nuptial bodies come home
to dye the birthing river scarlet.
what lies unsurmized 'neath a midden or
a mount of hair ignites the verity
of all distaff phenomena ... it added
in a telling parenthesis . it was
then he awoke and peering thru the leaves
beheld a giant red-breasted robin
pulling an earth-worm out of a topaz mountain
what lay under hand toucht blue sky

*

i had meant to write about a pear tree i knew as a child

when i lived over the mountains in a small prairie town but
the language of that pear tree belonged to my mother tongue . it
bespeaks a lost childhood language one which the pear tree in
our backyard in chinatown has a nodding acquaintance with .

how many languages does a pear tree speak ?

i am still sitting here trying to get a handle on my childhood
pear tree but all i can hear in its "ukiyoe" branches is
the voice of my mother as she bends over my head delicately lifting
tiny spoonfuls of wax from one pink ear then the other .
how many languages have i lost losing my childhood pear tree ...

and is it that loss that makes me the tongue-tied lover i be?

*

what i am given to "see" lies half-hidden

under the burdened keel buried in the pear tree's midden .
ask king solomon how he increast the pear tree's
yield by singing all night long up in its leafy branches .

in my book of hours : one forkt branch wraps itself
around a giant hour glass . while the other equally twisted
branch clasps our thronging bodies . what i am given
to "be" flies out of its midnight leaves ... utterly unseen

*

the pear tree a siamese cat named cooper and me

seem to have made a compact with these fall days –
one which has something to do with an improbable stiffening of
the ligaments and joints plus an oftimes acerbic-laugh
sandwicht between thin slices of callit-a-wanton-hunger
you said put a grey pallor on our relationship . unlike the other
two, i didn't want to admit to my infirmity . thus
the pear tree basks in the rotund sun striking my cheek while
stroking the fur of the paws-up-in-the-air siamese cat
lying on the light-struck carpet under my feet .
thus language – mirroring the eddys of our indiscretions –
deposits the trio and their common ailments at the
foot of the heapt-up midden . crumpled bent unrepentant

*

dear lesbia

– i'm thankful i didn't have to choose
between you and the pear tree though i must admit i
didn't think i'd have that choice made for
me : nor did i think of it as a deliberate intent on
your part til the very end when it became
impossible to tell "who" fell out of synch with "whom"
let alone "why" . bird bird of my once
fabled pear tree – there's one less song haunting
the morning alley since you flew off to
another nest in another neighbourhood . do fly by if
you have a spare wing and share a pear.
you know that i know a pear tree isn't anybody's property .
and if i may say so neither are you . nor i

*

thin sliver of november moon over maclean park

… i want to hang a thought on its silvery horn i want
it to illumine these disparate words : *words* i once thought
"you" and you alone made visible . incarnate in its very
origins we are the breath on which they fly … fly out of
the extremity of our winter solitude into another ear .
listen – "breath" bears the brunt of all the unstirr'd
silences to come : breath is a calling an actual reaching out .
ask the ode of an old pear tree who stopt listening …
                    – can you hear me from your tree?

*

just the other day i ate up the last bowlful of

your preserved pears and wasn't it just the day before
"yesterday" we stood in the back-alley looking up
at its array of white blossoms and under our breath say
how lucky we are to find such a splendid clapboard
house with its own tall pear tree . eight brimfilld years
spoke to me as i put the last sliver in my mouth and
suckt up all the sweet pear juice . from here on in i'll
have to go it alone if i'm to compost another spring .
i'll miss your preserved pears your paring knife and son .

p/s there's a dozen pears rotting on top of the camper

*

summer came and went leaving its traceries on his fall

if the pear tree didn't stand so tall outside the study window
he might well have gone off to bed thinking he had invented
its midnight-presciences for a small clandestine pome's sake . but
given the gift-of-sleep, with all its inchoate portends, the pear tree
crackled with forebodings nobody in their right minds would think
twice of repudiating. prophetic in its mastery of all the seasons
since the beginnings of speech it thinks with its whole being.
given the gift of its haunted syntax … these words rehearse
the music of "the last day of a certain year beyond which there
is nothing left of time." "nothing left to decline but the
divinity of air …" i thought i heard a bitten pear pray

*

belatedly, for kit's 11th birthday
midnight, may 13th '80

this house this small clapboard house we three thrive in is
mostly wood, paper and words – i sd to myself as i looked all a-
round me. this small house heapt with worlds on paper invites
even more paper and words to help themselves to a place on our
already crowded shelves – i thot as the very paper under my hand
filled up with words. this un-bored wood, paper and breath a-
bode beside a creek with a tall pear tree has no beginning middle
or ending – i caught myself saying to the wind as row on row of
perpendicular worlds tilted their paginations at my small feat.
built of wood breath and a thimbleful of words : this small house
simply, simply abides us

*

these words seem to be rehearsing –

the unquantifiable extinction of all similitudes …
i thot i heard a bitten pear say .
"stuff and nonsense" hisst a stern verb – tossing
love's pomposity higher than an april kite

o dance a jig on the pear tree's midden heapt
with divers wonderments . language is a fool's fruit
fool-proof pear trees bear the laughter of .
put your ear to its forkt-trunk – hear its sap thrum

*

in my day-break dream :
somebody in a fool's green costume was seen waving
2 luminous syllables by their
golden stems – shouting P-E-A-R-S! P-E-A-R-S!

– how come "you" turned out to be
the green fool with slender phosphorescent fingers
and i – the golden stems? How
does a pear tree circumvent mistaken-identities?

*

dear wallace stevens

— not til i got this far which is as far as
a handful of dried pear stems have brought me ... did i feel
the "pips" of your two pears implode in the loam of
my pear tree's midden heap . long before i ever thought to
write "them" your pears composted the night air . — if
these "auguries" to an old pear tree veer too far in the wind
of a disembodied wit ... i'm almost certain that you of
all the poets i read in my young manhood will indulge me with
a passing nod if not a handshake . i'll take a twang of
your "blue guitar" anyday of the week over reams of semiotic-
nonsense . language overload that obstructs the rush of
an intent speech bores the pear i be . permit it this screech

       yours, complete with worm holes

*

how to shake a ripe pear down

hop up and down on the branch it dangles from
til it drops. get fat-assed 'cause mean
winters comin' with lots of rain. whoever steps
on a fallen pear steps on a small bird's just dessert.
this is an old bird mocking the pecking order
of local politics. it's about all the stale white bread
and baloney sandwiches no pear tree bird in its
right mind would stoop to eat. it's about the absence
of love among the glistening towers and all the
inhospitable machines. "hava bite on me" sd
the providential pear tree to a migrant bird breasting
an unseasonable squalor. "holler if you need me"

*

– if on a cold winter morning you
fill up on a bowlful of ripe pears say "grace"
and praise the perennial mating of sol
and chlorophyll – this is the indigenous voice
of an old crow cawing up a commotion –

pears struck from the spoilage of a man's will often
emit a quantum of unalloyed noise ´

pears : persimmons : & pumpkins all got
their p's and s's loopt together into a sibilance
even if nothing else clings to them : this
is their contingency-plan their unplanned mandate
– this is the hiss of personification

listen – a dangling pear spinning a winter Omen says
let your own fruit drop ... and fast, again

*

thinking about all the eavesdroppers

e/g the poets / the birds up in the pear tree monitoring
the daily round-of-awe for a small pome's sake :

thinking about a "you" i once knew and your preserved pears
   "   "   about a small "me" and my pitiless fruit
   "   "   about all the frost-bitten pears hugging its hearth

the old midden in unsurpassing rhetorick proclaimed –
I COMPOST THE LANGUAGE-TREE:
                              TAKE YOUR CLUES FROM ME!

*

what i have been given to do will bear

its own felicities an ancient midden i've dreamt about
utterly enfolds . otherwise silences abound –
& the bounty is this hissing rain this whining midnight siren
& these my twice emptied-out clay hands . i would
write a cantata for a harp & a small bronze bell if i could
sound the unpeel'd silence when the last pear falls ....

*

moment-
arily air
borne

another
mottled pear
slides –

down
an unseen
draft

to touch
earth
home–free

*

there are no words left for

how i feel towards you : no words that haven't
returned to the well-of-silences .
if i told you that my feelings are grounded
in the still waters of my own body ...
would you believe me? would you have placed
your ear to my chest and listened?
the brilliant october air laves the back-alley
the pear tree lets its last leaves fall ....

there are no words left bearing the seasons of
a once fruitful tree – do you hear me?

*

there must be at least one pome to a pear tree in all

the divers tongues of the morning world pear trees thrive in.
i am simple – i want to believe that a sapling planted in
the loam of a pome will one day flower into a tall pear tree
bearing a basket full of fruit, indigent birds, and diligent
lovers of the marvelous. i want to consort with all the
bruised pears pitting the dew-lapt grass. in all the divers
tongues scoured by its first flowering : there's a scented
nomenclature breathing a votive Y-E-S! among its graven leaves.
o st francis! there's a full moon lighting up its thatch!

*

morning sun emblazons

the photograph of a family i once had
past-tense : past all pretence –
it shines in upon a once thriving nest

fate is a lengthening shadow an unwept
tear glistening a granular silver-
bromide print : what i beheld i became

*

in this our
one thousand nine hundred
eighty-second
            summer a.d.

in this our
summer of pitiless animosities the
chinese anglican church
of the good shepherd choir is singing
onward christian soldiers
marching as to war
in this our summer of nuclear fallout
and ekonomic depletion
in these and other
acts of psychological terrorism
teach us o wrathful one!
how to tend a small garden and
in its daily tending
learn (again! how to nurture
our impoverishment

will you forgive me for
seeming to make light of a bright
sunday morning service
but – the very hum of my typewriter
depends upon the sun's
electro-magnetic aplomb! and if i
may say so – so does your
gone-to-seed going-awry garden
full of pungent verbs

*

like the golden hub of an ancient
chinese chariot wheel : the spokes the branchings
of the fabled pear tree radiate out
over the roof-tops of my pacifica *hooping*
water earth air wood metal and fire

like the endless
column constantin brancusi
built to point a
finger at the bestial sun
these brine words
wave towards the pear
tree's trunk full
of intricate divinations

say "pear tree" twice if
you want a turn on a tall sky-wheel
say "pear tree" thrice if
you want a ride on an eagle's back with
a breath-taking view of
the whole turning/burning dream wheel

*

a capricorn pear tree

up / side / down   its
calligraphic-branches twist in
the fist of a winter-
wind into an uproaring of
knarled hands shaking –
a skyful of dread   in the face
of a wan winter moon .

what i am given to tell dwells
intact in a raven's eye

*

"the body i am is the purest instrumentation of desire i know"

sing—
the unslakt
heft
of
hunger

the
midden's
trove
of wonder-
ments

sing—
its
riddled
love
song

say
i love you
midden
heap of my
being

almost
"me"

*

who knows if i'll be around
when they come to chop my pear tree down
to build another condominium

magpie! magpie!
swayin' on a high silverbranch!
will you caw me —

if you catch a glimpse of the axe-
man comin' down our alley
cause i've got a petition signed by
all the neighborhood children
who haven't had a chance to skin their knees
let alone laugh and sneeze
up inside its thatched corridors
and there's a young couple
i know who want to build their first nest
in its forkt-branches

magpie! magpie!
will you be my unpaid informer ?
my unimpeachable i ?

*

long after the pear tree's final surge of sap …

these spare words shapt from a handful of dried pear stems
will rebirth (again) in a remote corner of your mind :
"where" the unnamed "breath" blew an unnamed "terror" into
the pith of a hapless "verb" and thus "death" got born

how many dawns stalk the pages of the book of etymologies?
how many nights has "it" used my addlepated tongue …

*

heapt with leaves the midden hides my mirth

mother
i am nothing but this
pod-of-breath
caressing its heapt-up
exuberance/s
nothing if not all
the mud twig
and spittle consonants
the whole air –
borne extravaganza!

mother the nests
we feather at speech's behest

*

pied
pear

i love
you

pith
stem

seed
un –

voiced
sun

*

dear pear tree

it's taken me 56 winters to cry real tears ....
how long do you think it'll take me to learn to die, clear-eyed?

ROBERT KROETSCH
DELPHI: COMMENTARY

: the calendar of *anthropos*
  is the clown-god's whip*

*It seems that from the
beginning the sanctuary
of Delphi has been the
object of innumerable
plots.*

  – Pausanias, 2nd
   Century A.D.

What can we say for certain?
The day was sure to be a clear
one; Meg reported that at break-
fast. She had, while her sister
was in the shower, taken a pic-
ture of the Parthenon. The
Hotel Herodion is under the
Acropolis. My room faced on
the walled garden where late-
night drinkers whispered in
various tongues to the grape vines and the waiters. Meg took a picture.
The window framed the picture she would take: high on the sunlit rock,
the Parthenon in profile to the August-morning light. I was drinking too
much coffee while my daughters, Laura and Meg, ate honeydew melon
and sampled the feta. We had not finished our eating when the driver
came into the breakfast room, his eyes naming us.

*fragment from "The Eggplant Poems"

:   the glyph on the broken stone
    raises the eye, reads the tongue

We were, it turned out, taking a bus to catch our bus.
We were the only passengers, my two American daughters
and I, until the driver stopped at
another hotel and a Japanese lady
came up the stairwell of the bus,
an elegant lady so small our greetings
went over her head. She was wearing a
soft white hat with two plastic buttons
pinned discreetly on the left side, one
of them reading, OUZO POWER. She had
brought along her smile. She put it
on. The streets of Athens were morning
streets; I wanted coffee at a sidewalk
cafe. But the driver thumbed his horn
at all of Constitution Square. We
turned into a side street. We were
unloaded from the bus, for sorting
according to language:

    Greek
    English
    German
    French
    Italian

Pausanias's Description of Greece,
translated with a commentary by J. G.
Frazer (Macmillan and Co., Limited,
St. Martin's Street, London, 1913):
*All the twenty-seven names of the Olympic
trophy occur on the Delphic trophy, but
the order is somewhat different, and on
the Delphic trophy there are four names
  … which, if Pausanias's list is
correct, did not appear on the Olympic
trophy. How are these discrepancies
to be explained?*

Lacedaemonians
Athenians
Corinthians
Tegeans
Sicyonians
Aeginetans
Megarians
Epidaurians
Orchomenians
Phliasians
Troezenians
Hermionians
Tirynthians
Plataeans
Thespians
Mycenaeans
Ceans
Melians
Tenians
Naxians
Eretrians
Chalcidians
Canadians
Styrians
Eleans
Potidaeans
Leucadians
Anactorians
Cythnians
Siphnians
Ambraciots
Lepreans

:   the chariot fell
    into the sky

and, going to Delphi, going to Delphi, I had expected
to ask a question, the three of us on the bus, the morning
ride, into morning, my daughters with me, there on the road
to Delphi

going to Delphi, a father, his two daughters

> Laura, entering college in
> the fall: We could ask if
> acid rain will dissolve the
> world, make it as pure as
> glass, as empty.

going to Delphi,
a question, seeking
a speaker

into a forest
of olive trees

going to Delphi

> and Margaret, to her father:
> Why do you want to be a tree?

I want to be an *olive* tree, I explained, not just any old
tree; one of those ancient olive trees, with holes clean
through the trunk, where you can see out the other side.
To what? Meg said. To other olive trees, I explained

going to Delphi

:   the /Pythian/ silence

and the voice on the loudspeaker system:

                  Marathon. That

place over there /that we've just passed, that you almost
saw/ is Marathon. The messenger, when the Persians were
defeated, ran all the way to Athens. They had no Key Tour
buses then /laughter/. He ran those twenty-two miles /the
precious words, locked on his tongue/. His message spoken
/the victory spoken, the city saved/ he fell down dead.

and the voice on the loudspeaker system:

                  Thebes. That

small town that you see just over there was once /famous,
I did not dare add, for its fresh water, for its abundance
of trees/ a city. It was leveled stone from stone by the
Macedonians /of Alexander the Great/.

and if   and when I fell asleep,
                    lulled by the bus, and my
                    head tilted and teetered,
                    almost fell off, Meg woke
                    me up with her

                    /daughterly/

                    giggling

and if
the /abandoned/
poem
speaks

:   silence   is a form of periphrasis

We stopped for coffee. The bus stopped. We filed out,
all of us, out of the bus, through categories of trade,
T-shirts, postcards, cups and saucers with pictures on
them of Mt. Parnassus.

I sat down, over coffee, under the big windows, by a woman
from Australia. She was in her late seventies, traveling
alone, alone for six weeks, in Europe. She praised the
beauty of my daughters. Her eyebrows were soft white
caterpillars that moved on her forehead when she spoke.
We talked of weather, of crops, the woman from Australia
and I. Her husband, long dead, had been a wheat farmer.
During the war, she explained, he had trained in Canada.
Aircrew. He had seen the wheatfields of Canada. He was
killed in a crash. That was her first husband. Her second
husband, he too was dead.

Pausanias, the ordinary
traveler, of whom Sir
James Frazer said: *Without
him the ruins of Greece
would for the most part be
a labyrinth without a clue,
a riddle without an
answer.*

What did he eat, along the
way? What drinks did he
stop for? Did he meet old
ladies who spoke to strangers
of husbands dead in the wars?
What was the road like,
without buses? Were the
washrooms clean? Did fathers
travel with their daughters,
and weep in the night for
love?

Pausanias, the ordinary
traveler:

(BK. VII ACHAIA, CH. XXIII, PT. I) *I have also heard say
that the water of the Selemnus is a cure for love in man
and woman, for they wash in the river and forget their
love. If there is any truth in this story, great riches
are less precious to mankind than the water of the Selemnus.*

: the holes in the cheese contain the cheese

And behind us, on the seats behind us, talking across the
aisle as we talked across the aisle, three women from New
Jersey: three braggart women, baggy-faced, rich-bitch
clothing and one of the three painted to look like a child,
all of them jangling their gold
in our ears, and asking each

Sir James Frazer: ... the other: How will we get our
Delphians decreed that for stuff through Customs? They
the future the oracles schemed and plotted, one
should be pronounced, not deciding which three blouses
by a virgin, but by a woman to wear through Customs,
over fifty years of age, another planning to fill her
attired as a virgin. brassiere (how will we get
our stuff through Customs?) with Turkish coins. They heard
from a conversation behind us that the site of Delphi is all
up and down, not level. We should have stayed in Athens
and gone shopping, they told each other. And my young
daughters looked daggers across the aisle to me, intending
their glances to swerve, become eagles, become thunder-
bolts ...

Sir James Frazer, in
response to Pausanias's
doubt (he believed in the
gods, in the heroes) as to
whether the Celts possessed
an art of divination
(X, XXI, 2):

The Celts practised divination by means
of human sacrifices; the victim was
stabbed in the back and omens were
drawn from his convulsions ... Justin
mentions that, before engaging in battle
with Antigonous, king of Macedonia, the
Gauls slew victims and drew omens from
their entrails.

: eat your breakfast before lunch;
    buy shoes for both feet

on the dangerous road to Delphi, Oedipus, King of Thebes:

The Cleft Way

From this point the high
road to Delphi grows
steeper and more difficult
to a man on foot. Many and
diverse are the tales told
about Delphi, and still
more about the oracle of
Apollo. (Pausanias. His
scattered Greece under
Roman rule.)

It is always that way, the poem, the abandoned poem, in
which the hero, seeking the answer to the impossible
question, seeking the impossible question, takes to the road.
Hero. Eros. The evasion that is the meeting. The impossible
road.

It is always that way.
Swing with the road's high
curve, upward, past the
bauxite mines (spilling the
mountain ochre and orange).
And the first glimpse, over
the fell and crisscross
hills, a gap, agape; and a
shaped stone (broken); and
on its slant of (shaping)
stone, under the sky-high
cliff:

The city of Delphi stands wholly on a slope, and not only the city, but also the sacred close of Apollo. The close is very spacious, and is situated at the highest part of the city … I will mention what seemed to me the most noteworthy of the votive offerings.

We blundered our way out of the bus,
into a line where we might buy tickets,
at seventy drachmas each, a ticket
blank on one side, on the other an
almost pale green, to the left in grey
and white a drawing of the head of
Socrates, balding, bearded; to the
right of the drawing, first in Greek,
then in English: YOU HAVE KILLED
O DANOI, THE MOST LEARNED
WHO EVER CAUSED GRIEF: THE
NIGHTINGALE OF THE MUSES,
THE VERY BEST OF THE GREEKS

The Sacred Way. We began
our ascent of the Sacred Way,
a letter "S" in reverse, ascending
the slope. We prepared to ascend
(we entered in); we found our
guide. *On entering the precinct
you see [*you do not see*] a bronze
bull made by Theopropus, an
Aeginetan, and dedicated by the
Corcyraeans. It is said that in
Corcyra a bull used to leave the
herd and the pasture to go down and bellow by the sea-
shore. The same thing happened every day, till the herdsman
went down to the shore and beheld a countless shoal of
tunnies. He told the Corcyraeans in the city, and they, after
laboring in vain to catch them, sent envoys to Delphi, and
in consequence they sacrificed the bull to Poseidon, and
immediately after the sacrifice they caught the fish; and
with the tithe of their take they dedicated the offerings at
Olympia and Delphi.*

:   the gnomon is all
      that remains

We were under a cliff. On the Sacred Way. The sloping
pathway, under a cliff. Meggie would take no pictures.
She wanted, first, her own silence, against the silence
of the cliff, as if even the sound of her camera might
snap that spur of Mt.
Parnassus down upon us,
that story, of Earth,
of Gaia, and her sacred
spring, and its guardian
serpent, and Apollo, the
new god, killing the   persons
serpent, killing his way   guilty of
into mercy, there, under   sacrilege
his temple   were

(we were climbing toward   flung
his temple; we stopped to
stare at the Treasury of   down the
the Athenians; we stopped (above)
to catch our breath)
                    cliff

the dark and underworld
force of the earth,   (Jack and
struck into a speaking   Jill went
splendor, into a prophetic, (quite a tumble
a singing, splendor

                    into the
                    Arkoudorema
                    (the Bear's
                    Gully

                    (belly)

After the hard questions we ask the question, What? What
did you say? And the wind blowing. And how the wind
came up, and the dust, I don't know. The wind was blowing.
The feet of the tourists powdered the dust. What was it I
said I said? I said to Laura.

the   Pausanias: *What the Delphians*
                                       call the Navel (omphalos) *is*
belly   *made of white marble, and is*
                                       said by them to be at the center
button   *of the whole earth, and Pindar*
                                       in one of his odes agrees with
of the world   *them.*

where two eagles

flying from the world's ends

met

(meet?)

Meggie was taking pictures. Laura and I stood behind the
omphalos and Meggie took a picture. Meggie and Laura
stood behind the omphalos and I took a picture. Meggie and
I stood behind the omphalos and Laura took a picture.

How does one pose for a   Frazer: *Even in his best days*
picture taken at the   *he [Apollo] did not always rise*
belly button of the earth?   *to verse, and in Plutarch's*
What smile is not a smile   *time the god appears to have*
of embarrassment? of   *given up the attempt in despair*
self-satisfaction? of   *and to have generally confined*
hybris? What angle of the   *himself to plain, if not lucid,*
arm does not betray a   *prose.*
certain inappropriate
possessiveness?

karpouzi:
watermelon

Only then did we realize,
we had lost our tour.

The Delphic letter E, cut into stone;
that is the mystery that no one can explain.

One day, one night, before Pausanias, before Socrates,
before Apollo (?)

the last person who knew what it means (what it meant)
perished.

That's the way it is.
The answer (or was it the question?):

                              mislaid?
                              stolen?
                              revised?
                              erased?
                              forgotten?
                              denied?
                              concealed?
                              replaced?
                              remembered?
                              laughed out
                              of court?
                              supposed
                              to be
                              sacrilegious?

watermelon is (not)
karpouzi

We went up the stone ramp, Laura and Meg and I. The floor, open to the sky was as bare as a granary floor in summer before harvest begins. Six pillars remain where Croesus, told that in waging a war against a great power he would destroy a great power, heard, but did not understand.

They say that the most ancient temple of Apollo was made of laurel, and that the boughs were brought from the laurel in Tempe. The temple must have been in the shape of a shanty. The Delphians say that the second temple was made by bees out of wax and feathers, and that it was sent to the Hyperboreans by Apollo ... As to the story that they made a temple out of the fern that grows on the mountains by twining the stalks together while they were still fresh and green, I do not admit it for a moment. Touching the third temple, it is no marvel that it was made of bronze, since Acrisius made a bronze chamber for his daughter ...

The wind was a dry wind.
There might have been
no sea at all, far below,
where the Pleistos River
winds its way through the
silver-green of olive
groves, out to blue
water. The dust was a
tight and grainy dust.

Frazer: *"a golden tripod resting on a bronze serpent* etc. "
A base which is believed to have supported this famous
trophy has been found by the French at the highest part of
the Sacred Way, to the east of the temple of Apollo ... The
bronze serpent on which the tripod rested is still to be
seen in the Almeidan, *the*
ancient Hippodrome, at
Constantinople, whither it
was transferred by
Constantine. The monument
consists really, not of a
single bronze serpent, but
of three such serpents so
skilfully intertwined that
their bodies appear as a
single spiral column, and
a very attentive
examination is necessary
to convince an observer
that there were actually
three serpents, not one.

"The Eggplant Poems," I
said, is a poem for which
we have no reliable text.
In fact, I haven't quite,
you might say, wrapped it
up. You mean, it doesn't
exist, Laura said. Now
wait a minute, I said. Is
there a difference between
a Greek poem which is lost
and a poem of mine which I
haven't been able to, for
whatever reasons, complete?

after I saw Apollo's temple I
wanted to turn back; I wanted
to turn down the hill again,
down the long (the sacred)
way; it was Meg who insisted
we climb on higher; it was
her idea, there in the dust; in
the pine forest, the cicadas:
Meg said, let's climb up
higher, past the theater (she,
pointing at the map in Laura's
book); and up we climbed,
higher, against the slope of
the mountain

Yes, Laura said. Yes, Meggie said. We have references to
the lost Greek poem, I presume, Laura said, or we wouldn't
know it once existed. True, I said. True enough. But I
can tell you about "The Eggplant Poems." The eggplant, I
might add, is closely allied to the potato. Both belong to
the nightshade family. As for the poem itself ...

I had missed the moment; the voice spoke and I was not
quite ready for my own hearing. I heard only the wind.
I was tired from the climbing, dusty, trying there to follow
after my young daughters. They leapt up the steep path.

The blown dust had closed my eyes. The cicadas were loud
in the pines. The pines smelled of their own sweating.
What I heard was a smaller sound, in the wind itself,
under the pulsing rhythm of the cicadas.

(The lost poem, *Margites*.
Homer's lost, satirical
epic, that comic poem
with a fool for its hero.
That lost poem that
might have changed
the warring world.)

(Sometimes,
high on a mountain,
one hears the lost poem.)

The voice reminded
me that it
had spoken. I
had heard it
there on the
temple floor while
I waited for
Meg to take
a picture. She
and Laura, together,
were studying the
(almost) vanished treasuries,
the Rock of
Sibyl. I had
noticed the olive
groves, on the
plain of Itea,
far below.

There is a rock rising above the ground. The Delphians say
that on this rock Herophile, surnamed Sibyl, used to stand
and chant her oracles ... The earlier Sibyl belonged, I
find, to the most ancient times. She is said by the Greeks

the mind
does not rhyme
with the hot wind;
          beware
any trick of
the eye.

Autobiographillyria.
That's a new word.

to have been a daughter of Zeus
and Lamia, daughter of Poseidon,
and to have been the first woman
who chanted oracles; and they
say that she was named Sibyl by
the Libyans. Herophile was
younger, but still even she is
known to have been born before
the Trojan war; and she foretold
in her oracles that Helen would
grow up at Sparta to be the bane

of Asia and Europe, and that Ilium would be taken by the
Greeks on her account. The Delians remember a hymn which
she composed on Apollo ... also she says sometimes that
she is Apollo's wedded wife, sometimes that she is his sister,
or again his daughter. These poetical statements she made
under the influence of frenzy and the inspiration of the god.

The cicadas in those pines. My daughters ahead of me. They had already found the stadium, the *stadion* that I had insisted was somewhere else, in my misreading of their map. They were ahead of me, farther up the mountain, out of sight.

this is what it is
to love daughters;
the cicadas sing;
the pine trees smell
of the green smell
of pine;
the tourists clamber
against the heat;
the steep trail opens
into the stone-edged
place where
horses ran

We had
passed the
temple, the
theater too
below us;
I had
no interest
in the
stadium, the
sacred games,
the lost
sound of
colliding chariots,
the blunt
wreckage of
so many
dreams, the
bones discovering
mortality.

I was surprised at my own answer when my daughters asked me what I had asked. They knew I had fallen behind to get on with my listening. Or should I say, my questioning? They, somehow, knew that. I was surprised when I offered my explanation. I didn't have a chance, I said. My father asked the question first.

What are you doing here?
my father said.
Did I teach you nothing?

It was his awkward stating
(his farmer's patient
voice)
of the wind's ecstasy.

It was the tripod
raised to the stars.

It was the long trip
rewarded and
recalled.

It was the guidebook
lost.

The smell of blood
in the dusty air.

And the last, high
scream
of the sacrificed
beast.

Only my two daughters, smiling in their skeptical delight:
their father had heard the oracle speak. They were so
pleased with me, already I was a story to tell their friends.
We sat down on the stone seats, in the stadium. I wanted to
rest. Do you know what? they would begin, they were
already beginning, to their smiling, amused, delighted
friends. Do you know what happened ...

And I, not leading, following after my tall, blonde daughters,
there in the hot Greek sun of that August day, I had heard
the speaking in the wind.

What are you doing here?
Did I teach you nothing?

Let's miss the bus, they said, my daughters. Let's stay.
We can get back, somehow, to Athens. They wanted to stay,
there in Delphi. The small hotels around the mountain's
corner. We had noticed them. The tavernas, promising a
night of wine.

          (The poet, strayed.
          The lost poem that
          had to be lost, or
          the world with it.

          (The rippled water
          rocks the moon.

          (A penny, like the sun,
          seen from a certain angle
          surely is round.

It was I who said, We've got to go.

They wanted to stay, my two daughters. The sun came
down from the tall cliff. We had not even been inside the
museum.

It was I who said, We've got to go.

DAPHNE MARLATT

TOUCH TO
MY TONGUE

The brain and the womb are both centres of consciousness, equally important.

H.D., *Thought and Vision*

Une femme inscrite en exterritorialité du langage. Elle expose le sujet comme on s'expose à la mort. Car il est question qu'elle vive.

Louise Cotnoir,
"S'écrire avec, dans et
contre le langage"

for Betsy

this place full of contradiction

a confusion of times if not of place, though you understood when i said no not the Danish Tearoom – the Indonesian or Indian, was in fact that place of warm walls, a comfortable tarot deck even the lamps pick up your glow, a cabin of going, fjords in there, a clear and pristine look the winds weave through your eyes i'm watching you talk of a different birth, blonde hair on my tongue, of numbers, nine aflush with capuccino and brandy and rain outside on that street we flash down, laughing with no umbrella, i see your face because i don't see mine equally flush with being, co-incidence being together we meet in these far places we find in each other, it's Sappho i said, on the radio, always we meet original, blind of direction, astonished your hand covers mine walking lowtide strands of Colaba, the lighthouse, Mumbai meaning great mother, you wearing your irish drover's cap and waiting alive in the glow while i come up worrying danish and curry, this place full of contradiction – you know, you knew, it was the one place i meant.

houseless

i'm afraid, you say, are you? out in the wintry air, the watery sun welling close behind your shoulders i am following, the already known symmetry of your body, its radiant, bow-woman arched over me, integrity straight as an arrow. blind with joy i say oh no, thinking, how could i fear with you?

and now it's dark in here, deep, my cave a house, you on the other side of the country, our country of sea with the wind blowing, our country of reeds and grasses under unfathomed sky. i huddle small, i call you up, a tiny point of light, memory small like a far-off hole – are you there? in all this smoke, fear, images torn from the wall requiring life for a life / that she take it all, mother of giving turned terrible mother, blood-sipper, sorrow Durga. turning her back, she takes back what she gives, as you might, or i might. giving myself up to fear. turning away (for "safety's" sake).

there are no walls. fear / love, this light that flashes over the sea surrounding us. signals danger, yes, my house no house. i can only be, no vessel but a movement running, out in the open, out in the dark and rising tide, in risk, knowing who i am with you –

creatures of ecstasy, we have risen drenched from our own wet grasses, reeds, sea. turned out, turned inside out, beside ourselves, we are the tide swelling, we are the continent draining, deep and forever into each other.

yes

JADE a sign on the road announces, *ijada, piedra de*, stone of that space between the last rib and the hipbone, that place i couldn't bear the weight of his sleeping hand upon – and my fingers flutter to my ring, gone. only a white band the skin of years hidden under its reminder to myself of the self i was marrying – "worthless woman, wilful girl." standing athwart, objecting, "so as to thwart or obstruct," "perversely." no, so as to retain this small open space that was mine.

perverse in that, having to defend myself from attack, encroachment on that soft abyss, that tidal place i knew as mine, know now is the place i find with you. not perverse but turned the *right* way round, redefined, it signals us beyond limits in a new tongue our connection runs along.

you call me on the phone, have you lost something? and i startle yes. half of it is here, you say. not lost, not lost. broken open on my finger, broken open by your touch, and i didn't even feel a loss, leaving the need for limits at your place, leaving the urge to stand apart i sink into our mouths' hot estuary, tidal yes we are, leaking love and saying it deep within.

coming to you

through traffic, honking and off-course, direction veering, presently up your
street, car slam, soon enough on my feet, eager and hesitant, peering with the
rush of coming to you, late, through hydrangeas nodding out with season's
age, and roses open outline still the edge of summer gone in grounding rain.
elsewhere, or from it, i brush by, impatient, bending to your window to sur-
prise you in that place i never know, you alone with yourself there, one leg on
your knee, you with boots, with headphones on, grave, rapt with inaudible
music. the day surrounds you: you point where everything listens. and i slow
down, learning how to enter – implicate and unspoken (still) heart-of-the-world.

kore

no one wears yellow like you excessive and radiant storehouse of sun, skin smooth as fruit but thin, leaking light. (i am climbing toward you out of the hidden.) no one shines like you, so that even your lashes flicker light, amber over blue (*amba*, amorous Demeter, you with the fire in your hand, i am coming to you). no one my tongue burrows in, whose wild flesh opens wet, tongue seeks its nest, amative and nurturing (here i am you) lips work towards undoing (*dhei*, female, sucking and suckling, fecund) spurt/ spirit opening in the dark of earth, *yu!* cry jubilant excess, your fruiting body bloom we issue into the light of, sweet, successive flesh . . .

eating

a kiwi at four a.m. among the sheets green slice of cool going down easy on the
tongue extended with desire for you and you in me it isn't us we suck those
other lips tongue flesh wet wall that gives and gives whole fountains inner moun-
tains moving out resistances you said ladders at the canyon leap desire is its way
through walls swerve fingers instinct in you insist further persist in me too wave
on wave to that deep pool we find ourselves/it dawning on us we have reached
the same place "timeless" you recognize as "yes" giving yourself not up not in
we come suddenly round the bend to it descending with the yellow canyon flow
the mouth everything drops away from time its sheets two spoons two caved-
in shells of kiwi fruit

climbing the canyon even as

the Fraser rushes out to sea and you, where you are i am, muddy with heart-
land silt beside the river's outward push my car climbs steadily away from and
toward – where we were – each step we took, what you said, what i saw (sun in
your hair on the rim of your look), smell of love on our skin as we rushed with
the river's push out, out to the mouth taking everything with us / and away, as
i leave you there (where i am still) to make this climb i don't want to, feel how
it hurts, our pull, womb to womb, spun thin reaching Sailor's Bar, Boston Bar,
reaching Lytton where the Thompson River joins, alone nosing my way into
the unnamed female folds of hill, soft sage since we came down twelve days
ago begun to bloom, gold and the grass gold, and your hair not gold but like
as light shivers through these hills. i am waiting for the dark, waiting with us at
Ashcroft, behind glass, by the river's edge: then going down to it, that bank of
uncertain footing as the freight roars by, across, that black river in its rush,
noisy, enveloping us as we envelop each other – and the wind took your hair
and flung it around your look, exultant, wild, i felt the river pushing through,
all that weight of heartlocked years let loose and pouring with us out where
known ground drops away and i am going, beyond the mountains, past the
Great Divide where rivers run in opposite direction i am carrying you with
me.

prairie

in this land the rivers carve furrows and canyons as sudden to the eye as if
earth opened up its miles and miles of rolling range, highway running to its
evercoming horizon, days of it, light picking flowers. your blackeyed susans are
here, my coral weed in brilliant patches, and always that grass frayed feathery
by the season, late, and wild canada geese in the last field. i imagine your blue
eye gathering these as we go, only you are not here and the parched flat opens
up: badlands and hoodoos and that river with dangerous currents you cannot
swim, TREACHEROUS BANK, sandstone caving in: and there she goes,
Persephone caught in a whirlwind the underside churns up, the otherwise of
where we are, cruising earth's surface, gazing on it, grazing, like those 70 mil-
lion year old dinosaurs, the whole herd browsing the shore of Bearpaw Sea
which ran all the way in up here, like Florida, she said, come in from the
desert region they were hungry for grass (or flowers) when something like a
flashflood caught them, their bones, all these years later, laid out in a whirlpool
formation i cannot see (that as the metaphor) up there on the farthest hoodoo,
those bright colours she keeps stressing, the guy in the red shirt, metal flash-
ing, is not Hades but only the latest technician in a long line of measurers.
and earth? i have seen her open up to let love in, let loose a flood, and fold
again, so that even my fingers could not find their way through all that bush,
all that common day rolling unbroken.

hidden ground

lost without you, though sun accompanies me, though moon and the maps say always i am on the right track, the Trans-Canada heading east – everything in me longs to turn around, go back to you, to (that gap), afraid i'm lost, afraid i've driven out of our territory we found (we inhabit together), not *terra firma*, not dry land, owned, along the highway, cleared for use, but that other, lowlying, moist and undefined, hidden ground, wild and running everywhere along the outer edges. lost, *losti*, lust-y one, who calls my untamed answering one to sally forth, finding alternate names, finding the child provoked, invoked, lost daughter, other mother and lover, waxing tree, waist i love, water author sounding the dark edge of the words we come to, augur- ess, issa, lithesome, *lilaiesthai*, yearning for you, and like a branch some hidden spring pulls toward our ground, i grow unafraid increasing ("lust of the earth or of the plant"), *lasati*, (she) yearns and plays, letting the yearning play it out, playing it over, every haystack, every passing hill, that tongue our bodies utter, woman tongue, speaking in and of and for each other.

where we went

we went to what houses stars at the sea's edge, brilliant day, where a metal crab jets water catching light, heaven and earth in a tropic embrace joined upright, outside glass doors people and cars and waterglaze. city that houses stares, city that houses eyes, electricity writing the dark of so many heads figuring where we were. we knew so well i didn't even catch your eye as we stepped through and she brought out the rings for us to look at, silver, moon metal engraved in the shape of wild eyes by kwakiutl and haida hands, raven and wolf and whale and unknown birds not seen in the light city. creatures of unorganized territory we become, a *physical impulse* moving from me to you (the poem is), us *dancing in animal skins* in the unmapped part of our world. now you wear whale on the finger that enters and traces in whale walrus the horse you thought i was, shy of fences, running the edge of the woods where brought up short i feel the warmth of you, double you, wolf. i wear wolf and dream of your lean breast descending, warm and slow the fur that grows between your eyes fifteen hundred miles away in another city under the same moon.

down the season's avenue

sunrise 7:18, sunset 7:23: we are approaching that point when the pivot of dawn and the pivot of night balance the narrowing day. you in it far off on the coast climbing what tree over the sea to gaze east? everywhere i see light lean along a curved plain. no intimate clefts of earth, no hilly rise but plain ("flat, clear") under the eye of horizon, that boundary you are on the other side of, two hours earlier. flat, *plano-*, plain as the palm of my hand, but i can't see. i try the trees for company, these lives, leaves, sudden against their going, lucid and startled. i ride their coming into view, not knowing, whispering where are you? down the avenue your breath runs up my spine, you shiver through, clear as the fire in turning leaves, clear as your voice that lights i'm here, clear as that point when the plane comes in and you will be standing there. i'm coming home.

in the dark of the coast

there is fern and frost, a gathering of small birds melting song in the under-brush. close, you talk to one. there is the cedar slant of your hair as it falls gold over your shoulder, over your naked, dearly known skin – its smell, its an-swering touch to my tongue. fondant, font, found, all that melts, pours. the dark rain of our being together at last. and the cold wind, curled-up fronds of tree fern wanting touch, our fingers separate and stiff. we haven't mourned enough, you say, for our parting, lost to each other the last time through. in the dark of this place, its fire touch, not fern but frost, just one of the houses we pass through in the endless constellation of our being, close, and away from each other, torn and apart. i didn't know your hair, i didn't know your skin when you beckoned to me in that last place. but i knew your eyes, blue, as soon as you came around the small hill, knew your tongue. come, you said, we slid together in the spring, blue, of a place we'd been. terra incognita known, *geysa*, gush, upwelling in the hidden Norse we found, we feel it thrust as waters part for us, hot, through fern, frost, volcanic thrust. it's all there, love, we part each other coming to, geyser, spouting pool, hidden in and under separate skin we make for each other through.

coming up from underground

out of the shadows of your being, so sick and still a shade under it, your eye looks out at me, grave and light at once, smiling recognition. draw close, i am so glad to see you, bleak colour of your iris gone blue, that blue of a clear sky, *belo*, bright, Beltane, "bright-fire." draw me in, light a new flame after your sudden descent into the dark. draw me close so i see only light your eye a full moon rides, *bleikr* in the old tongue, shining, white, ascent above horizon fringed with black reed, horsetail, primitive flicker on the rim of eons ascending this white channel we wander in, a plain of "wild beestes" felt at the periphery of vision, fear and paranoia ready to spring – beyond the mind or out of it they say, though "defended … with apparent logic." in this landscape we are undefended in the white path of our being, lunar and pulled beyond reason. *bleikr*, shining white, radiant healing in various bright colours, *blanda*, to mingle and blend: the blaze of light we are, spiralling.

healing

stray white lips, petals kissing middle distance between blue iris you, me, moss there and small starred dandelions. in the drift gathering, days, hours without touch. gauze, waiting for the two lips of your incision to knit, waiting for our mouths to close lip to other lip in the full spring of wet, revived, season plants come alive. this season of your body traumatized, muscles torn where the knife went, a small part of you gone. gall, all that is bitter, melancholy.

each day we climb a small hill, looking. rufous hummingbirds dive before our very eyes kissing space. fawn lilies spring moist lips to wing filled air. i want to open you like a butterfly. over bluffs at the rim of blue distance we might leap, free fall, high above us four bald eagles scream for pure glee. glee, it falls on us, bits of sound shining, rain of rung glass. glisten, glare. (g)listen, all of it goes back shining, even *gall* does, glass and glazing, every yellow hope a spark, lucid and articulate in the dark i wake to, reaching for you. somewhere a bird calls. it is our bird, the one that wings brightness, *springan*, scattering through us as your lips open under mine and the new rain comes at last, lust, springs in us beginning all over again.

Notes

this place full of contradiction

Mumbai is the vernacular name for Bombay, after the Koli goddess Mumbai (derived from Maha Amba, Great Mother). According to L.F. Rushbrook Williams in *A Handbook for Travellers in India, Pakistan, Nepal, Bangladesh and Sri Lanka*, she is the tutelary deity of this island, once seven islands separated at high tide, drained and reclaimed by the British. The southernmost tip is the site of the Colaba lighthouse.

houseless

Durga, or Kali, "the 'Unapproachable' and 'Perilous,'" is the deadly aspect of the goddess who is also World Mother (Jagad-Amba). See Erich Neumann, *The Great Mother*, pp. 151-2.

yes

piedra de ijada or "stone of the flank" is the Spanish name for jade, once believed to be a cure for kidney disease. "Jade" has also been used (by men) as a denigratory term for a woman.

kore

the story of Persephone's abduction by Hades and her subsequent reunion with Demeter is uniquely the story of the relationship between daughter (kore, maiden) and mother (De-meter, earth mother). It forms the heart of the rituals celebrated at Eleusis. "It was her own daughter who was buried under earth, and yet the core of *herself* died with her and came back to life only when Persephone – flower sprout, grain sprout – rose again from the earth." Nor Hall, *The Moon and the Virgin*, p. 83. "Every woman's womb, the mortal image of the earth mother, Demeter … " J. J. Bachofen, *Myth, Religion, and Mother Right*, p. 80.

dhei is the Indo-European root of "female" and means "to suckle" but has diversified into *fetus* (offspring, that which sucks), *fellatio* (sucking) and *felix* (fruitful, happy).

yu is the Indo-European root of "you," second person pronoun; also an outcry as in Latin *jubilare*, "to raise a shout of joy" (as the initiates at Eleusis might have done on seeing the luminous form of the risen Kore).

hidden ground

affiliate words for "lust" are Old Norse *losti* (sexual desire), Gothic *lustus* (desire), Greek *lilaiesthai* (to yearn), Sanskrit *lasati* (he yearns, he plays).

-ess is of course the English suffix indicating the female, derived from Latin *issa*.

where we went
the poet Alexandra Grilikhes, in an article entitled "Dancing in Animal Skins," speaks of reading poetry to an audience as a shamanic act: "the poet dances in animal skins to evoke in you what longs to be evoked or released"; "the speaking of poetry is above all a physical impulse, and the performance of the poem *is* the poem."

coming up from underground
"bleak" derives from Old Norse *bleikja*, white colour, rooted in Indo-European *bhel-* with its powerful cluster of meanings and associations: to shine, flash, burn, shining white and various bright colours, fire; *belo-*, bright, Beltane (the Celtic May Day festival celebrated with bonfires burning on the hills), Old Norse *bleikr*, shining, white, and *blanda*, to mingle and blend.

healing
the etymology of "gall" as in gallstone is interesting; it goes back to Indo-European *ghel-*, to shine, spawning words for colours, bright materials and bile or gall in a range from Germanic *gelwaz* (yellow) to Greek *khole* (bile, from which we get melancholy) to Germanic *gladaz* (from which we get glad), *glasam* (glass, glaze), Middle Dutch *glisteren* (shine), Old English *gleo* (glee).

DAVID MCFADDEN
COUNTRY OF THE OPEN HEART

Only a little man, one of those emasculated dancers who sudden-
ly spring up from behind bottles of white brandy, said sarcasti-
cally in a very low voice: "Viva Paris!" As if to say: "Here we do
not care for ability, technique or mastery. Here we care for some-
thing else."

Lorca

1

When the phone rings in the middle of the night
The toes of angels curl like pigs' tails,
Long-term vegetarians long for raw slabs of bacon
And a naked voice enters the head, a voice from the
Mountains that encircle the lives of solitary dreamers,
And the voice is as soft as the core of the heart,
The faithful molten centre of voluptuous art,
A voice so human the chips (with gravy) fall
Into the polonaise sauce of daily life
And the heart somersaults into silence
At the surprise eruption of its own inhumanity
And the murdered beauty of the loveliest life
On a Friday night in 1975 at the Cecil Hotel
In cold rainy downtown Vancouver with seven salesmen
Sitting at a table heavy and wet with beer and sweat.
But talk shifted to colour and it became apparent
All seven were at least partially colourblind.
And the talk turned to aging and it became apparent
All seven had been born on the same day
And each was celebrating his fortieth birthday.

The phone rings in the middle of the night.
The dreamer's heart is wearing a transparent bikini.

2

The dog stood on the bark, burning,
In the oceanic night of deliberate oil spills.
The dog picked up the pipe and puffed it,
The dog was discovered reading Pascal
And drowned in two inches of rainwater
While squirrels and cats refused to help
And his last thoughts were of you, tied
To a television antenna, your limbs

So long and white and leathery in the rain
And amid the thunder and lightning your voice:
"Don't forgive them, they know what they're doing."
From up there you saw the sea become as calm as a clam
As the murderous mob embarked for paradise
For their first return in three thousand years
But they found it had lost its rustic charm
And this kind of sentiment is an affliction
Reminiscent of the kind of person who can fall
Down a flight of stairs without spilling a drop
Of his mind. "So this is paradise, eh?
Be a nice place if they ever get drunk
On the spirit of the age and punch holes in the
Invisible wings of truck-driving dreamers,
Cut down a few of those overbearing trees,
Straighten out those crooked roads of genius."

3

Hands up those with hairy armpits.
Your heart is being torn in twain
By the banks of the river of the transparent
Self which has perfected the freedom to say
Anything but what it really wants to say.
Whatever became of Catullus' yacht?
All energy comes from desire's reversal
Said Venus to Adonis long ago
(Of course Adonis really said it to Venus
But it doesn't scan) (another reversal)
And the human race has awakened and now
Must reverse itself and fall asleep again –
The grapefruit tastes so wonderful
Between mouthfuls of fresh lobster –
And the holy trees still long to resume
Their impregnation of would-be tyrants
For whom time itself travels in reverse,

Waves crashing out from barbaric shores
Like radio signals from frantic planets,
Shrinking into the past with vast intelligence
And the knowledge that nothing need be known,
Crushed spiders becoming whole again
And shrinking into tiny eggs,
Drowning in a sea of ordinary light,
Apes drowning in a sea of butter,
Lions and tigers in a tidal wave of cream,
Giraffes saved by their long sweetheart necks.

The gibbons are butchering each other
At the far end of the jungle;
Their hairy dead bodies like sleeping swamis
Litter the beach between jungle and sea
Of soured buttermilk. Fate hath a way
Of providing such incredible spectacles,
And during the hostilities lobster
Will not be available unless an unusually
Adventurous gibbontrepreneur dares the trip
Through the holocaust to the creamy constant shore.
No plans have been made to chronicle this war.

And the river that runs through the center
Of the jungle where peace-loving tribes
Of gibbons toss grapefruit at each other
Is stained with piss and grapefruit juice
And their fabulous music never ends
Or just when you think it's about to end
A DC-10 crashes in downtown Toronto
And your doctor informs you a giant tapeworm
Has formed a cave in the centre of your brain
With care, with attention to all the details,
With obvious permanence in mind,
And is sucking at the backs of your eyeballs
As if they were memory glands
Lowing with spurts of optical milk aglow

In creation's instant midnight of typewriters.
And the reader's attention stretches lazily
At the centre of a hollowed-out modern romance
And he dreams of the carnage on the beach
Or the hollowed-out centre of Toronto.

4

The heart hath a handle in hell
And holds in its lap a bowl of constant cream
That changes its poisonous savour with the changing
Tides of fashion but the blood that flows
In all directions through time's hemispheres
Has its own knowledge of ecstasy and terror
Unrelated to such frivolous concerns:
Thus in the sea, when tides are strongest,
The surface often shows its calmest face
And the agony of cruel crucifixion
Lies behind the saint's beatific smile
As your writing, when it appears to be
Pretending to reflect spiritual truth,
Is merely moving through the nature of itself
Like a snake awakening on a mild spring morning.

Everybody notices everything, but no one
Who hath not a heart in hell's constant cream
Can understand the breakdown of the world,
Or the incessant cursing of the mind's unhappiness
In the surprise of the world's merriment.
An open heart is a joy entirely
And is enough to float a mighty thought
Or a mighty fleet of little thoughts
For under its furry red jacket
The heart is a fierce little mole
That can burrow forever in any direction
And change its course with the lightest thought

– So light it can never touch itself
And its very existence can't be detected.
Welcome to the country of the open heart.
Virginia is for lovers. Hospitality spoken here.
Concerto for lover, flute and harp.
Once open never to be closed again.

5

The rediscovery of paradise was billed
As the Canine Caper of the Century
And why not? The entire Pacific Ocean
Is a Spanish onion and you've never
Found it difficult to say where one ocean
Begins the day with a hearty breakfast
And the other seldom fasts at all.
While the hounds of heaven guard hell's gates
And yelp and yowl with almost human glory
The ocean begins to throb with devotion,
The naïve saloonkeeper asks Mae West
To sing for him, you want your every song
To be pregnant with the ecstasy of the age
(For to sing is to enter the Western
Gates of Paradise where heavenly hounds
Do shake the darling buds of Mae
If not the aging or even the aged)
And in the planetarium of heavenly pop bottles
A one-eyed lady sings a song about a total
Eclipse of the moon and expresses sweet regret
That she and her lover would probably be dead
Before the next one and you, uncharacteristically,
Said: "Heck, the way I'm going I'll be lucky to see
Halley's Comet," and later your cousin Fred
While on a night flight from Vancouver to Toronto
Noticed a vertical line in the sky –
On one side of the line the sky was dark

And on the other side light – and just then
The pilot announced the scientific name
For the phenomenon and described it as
"The line that separates night from day."
So on the next flight Fred stayed awake
Deliberately all night long looking for that line
But it failed to appear, and having forgotten
The scientific name for that most essential
Of all lines, he wrote a note to the pilot:
"What do you call the line
That separates night from day?"
And the pilot sent a note back saying
"I don't know what you're talking about."
– Just think of this story as a contribution
To the notion of contribution, an executioner
In a black hood full of inexpressible delights
Singing a lullaby to himself while awaiting victims,
A chronicle of Empty Lives and civilized brutality
And the road to hell is paved with dead dogs
And maybe the occasional dead cat.

This is your Empty Lives report
For Monday, May 28, 1979 – but first
A word from the bottom of the open heart.
Howdy, strangers. Do you sometimes feel
Empty Lives passing through your Open Heart?
Not nice, is it? Well, we have the answer.
Tell it to the Lord in prayer. This message
Is from the Open Heart Pornography Co-operative
Where you can find the finest in new and used passion,
Thoughtless people stomping on your tenderest memories,
Rabble-rousing racists raving about recent race riots,
And incestuous denials of wrongdoing in low places.
A ridge of Empty Lives is moving across
The Sechelt Peninsula bringing feelings of
Depression and hopelessness to the area.
Record suicide rates have been reported

In Bay St. John and Two Lips County
 — Even these lines are about to commit suicide
To protest in advance their lack of readers
And their inability to continue on forever
In a universe of their own deconstruction
For it's impossible to imagine a time or place
When or where anything that exists didn't.
This applecore stems from Incredible Woe
And what is your loneliness but the planet's?
And if you think this is pathetic
You should have seen the first draft!
You are watching a heart grown wild and strange,
A heart of suddenly inexplicable rhythmic patterns,
A heart of gradual basic coquetry sublime
And that heart is your sole possession
And don't think your friends don't admire
The calm detachment with which you observe
Your heart's grotesque configurations,
For its attempts to protest its sufferings
And the cruelty of the age in which it lives
And its attempts to assert its lost glory
And its attempts to rebel against its fate
And achieve victory over that ever-popular
Stand-up comedy team of Death and Death
Are, at best, half-hearted.

6

The blood that was used to boil the skulls
Flows in every conceivable direction
In the country of the open heart
Where cats and dogs discuss the weather
And there are as many ways of fearing
Death as there are of dying.
You may plunge forward courageously
Into the madness of your life

But the sky is full of snakes
And you're paralyzed by theoretical
Considerations of human freedom
For a snake is a long line of perfect verse,
There are no adjectives in heaven,
You don't know who to love and the open
Heart is a spreading pool of boiling grease.

Fall away from sin and grief
For your mind is the heart of the land of your birth,
Said the sea as it pounded away at transparent hearts
With the rhythms of sleazy 1950ish surrealism
And the heart is a flame the damned can love
With a desperate passion that vanishes with the world,
The question of doubt never coming to climax –
All over the world the sound of corks
Popping and dust rising on country roads.
Is this folk music? Can a glass
Of ordinary red blood be set to music?
There is nothing that cannot be planted
But thinking makes it grow, this wisdom,
The only wisdom worth living for,
The wisdom of the wind from the heart,
The wined wind that will never wind down,
The unwound heart, the wound-down heart,
And the heart that can never be wounded.

The autopsy showed a bottle of wine
Had somehow lodged in your heart.
Probable cause of death: poor vintage.
Forever drawing back from that final drink,
Civilization itself is the perfect epicurean.
You refused to drink to excess so your cousin Fred
Bonked you with a bottle of Vichy water.
(Would you be annoyed if someone picked up
A raisin from the floor and dropped it in your
Steaming plate of beef haiku and spinach?)

When ten million people start writing poems
Someone is bound to write something like this.
He told you to count your blessings and try
To live one day at a time and you
Set fire to yourself in the village square.

7

The heart is a power dam on that network
Of thick black blood flowing in all directions
Without motive, while the angels, their spread wings
Invisible as music of the future, as energy
Which lifts and lightens heaviest woe,
As the sadness of beautiful animals
And trees and discarded artifacts undreaming
In dim corners of the studied human earth,
Likewise fly in all directions, magnetism as real
As a blackberry bush, knowing itself only to be
Part of a music it will never hear.
A blood-boiled human skull sitting in the dump,
Tourists indulging in silly arguments,
The skull's eyes empty as opal rings,
And the skull waddles away as cameras click,
Flooding the future with unfocussed images,
And someone throws a beer bottle at the skull
And someone sticks a cigar butt in the blowhole
Of a trapped whale and the skull turns with sudden
Fear and runs smack into a wall of rock like a
Romantic stuck in the middle of a modern romance
And before the tourists' dull cameras and sharp eyes
The skull transforms itself into a mountain goat
And scampers straight up to the first ledge,
Glances down, then climbs straight up to the second
And the sun goes down and the moon comes up
And the tourists strip and start howling like gibbons

Unburdened of humanity's impossible woe
By an extremely rare convergence of stars,
Skull and mountain goat, dangerous
As a dream impossible to remember
In the open country of deathless art
Where love occasionally travels in reverse
So that it starts sour and ends sweet
And becomes more and more intense till it suddenly
Disappears like a butterfly unpinning itself
In the window of a Chinatown gift shop.

A tale told by the King of Burgundy
Who owns all the whales in the Western Sea:
Three ugly nuns – perhaps the ugliest
In all Christendom – were walking along
The lonely road from Aix-en-Provence
Where they were accosted by a strange creature,
Half bear, half goat, who began
Pestering them with terrible jokes about nuns.
"Why do they call them nuns? None better.
Haw haw haw," he bellowed, obnoxiously,
Slapping them on their backs with all his might
And breathing foul bear breath in their faces.
Then, as if that weren't bad enough:
"Three nuns are sitting in the tub," he said.
"One says where's the soap? Second says
I don't know. Third says sure does.
Haw haw haw haw." Oh, he was hawful!
And the nuns suddenly stripped off their habits
And showed they were really men in disguise,
Robbers seeking safe passage to Marseilles,
And they abused that foul half-bear half-goat
Mercilessly and left him half-dead in the road.

8

A dog is barking in the Garden of Eden
Where the swans and the blueberry honk and bloom,
Vainglorious reality is covered with moth eggs
And time is an omelet ready to fold.
The animals on other continents
Have perfected intricate patterns of war
But here the palm trees are amazed at their rapid
Development of dreaded self-consciousness.
Imagine, if you will, a sad old palm tree
Singing "Don't get around much any more"
Accompanied by Blueberry Bush on tin whistle.
This is a song to sadden the gladdest heart
Though it won't get you anywhere important. This
Is modern romance at its best, a veritable sex killer's
Vision of the annual picnic at the orphanage:
Enough undiluted sperm to float a boatload of roses
Along the River of Broken Hearts and Dreams
Where each glistening drop of sparkling dew
Is a perfect little human being
Waiting to be wakened into bliss
Or simply awakened by, for instance, a sentimental
Laser beam aimed at the tiny perfect opal
Suspended in a pocket of tears at the centre of the
Heart, the heart opening into the country of its birth,
A country overrun by angelic warlords
And swept daily by golden firestorms
Proven by independent research agencies
Using narrow-spectrum occurrence computers
To possess a malevolent form of intelligence
And a subtly childlike sense of humour.
The blackberry bush flowed in all directions.

Oh how fast these lines are running –
Lines for filthy minds, written by a lonely
Bar of soap melting in a pool of bath-tears.

One cannot claim authorship for a vague
Intuition that if one continues reading / writing
Something wonderful will happen.
You will receive a wonderful surprise.
That small tingling sensation will gradually grow
And your heart will begin to pound like butter
And you, my love, will turn into a blackberry bush
And your eyes will open and you will find
All as it was when your eyes were closed
For this is the country of the open eye
Where Shelley's glaciers stare at you like snakes
And the sky with a sigh is about to defame your name
And nature ropes its way around your neck
Like the tail of an unrecallable nightmare beast
Whose grey flesh rolls like tidal bores
Over rank after rank of transparent soldiers:
The Light Brigade, country of open sores.
For every day you make things, except for the days
You steal things, and every time you write a bad line
A cancer patient somewhere goes into remission
And every time you write a good line someone dies
And goes to heaven where every day
Is like today. It must have been wonderful
To have lived in Tahiti before those gangs of Gauguins
Came over the horizon like little lines of
Brilliant verse. Everything was taken care of
Though it would have been better if nature had put
A nice fresh fish inside each coconut.

The blackberry bush of naked nuns
Is flooded with images of a mind peeled
Like a skull in boiling blood, and a heart pure
And thoughtless as a dog's tongue panting
In the heat of a passing passion
And you shake the dog off your embarrassed leg
And scold it, saying: "You bad dog –
You don't see me carrying on like that,"

And you are astonished as the dog starts talking
In a California accent even though it's a Labrador
And it says: "When I heard that women were more
Emotional than men I burst into tears."

9

When it comes to the end of its current tragedy
The human heart opens as calmly as a clam
And squirts you in the eye. When you come
To the end of a perfect night you'll find
A Sleeping Princess with tiny naked breasts
And tiny naked breaths and you say what the heck
And you kiss her and she wakes up screaming
And the cops come and take you away.
The nice cop says he knows you from somewhere
And you cry because he reminds you of your dad.
In fact you're crying a lot these days.
You look at a falling leaf and cry.
You see a man walking down the street
With a violoncello and you cry. You know
You'll die without ever playing like Rostropovich.
You remember catching leaves as a child.

Night falls and the heart shudders in its sleep.
Someone has filled the teapot with gravy.
A cat named Buddy is crying at the back door.
He is not worried about the fate of the world.
He doesn't even care if I finish this stanza.
Or, if I do, if you do, my dainty monsters.

But at the death of the Queen of Burgundy
The hearts of many shuddered in the sweet
Light of dawn. Oh the agony. Can she really
Be gone? For the greatest fear is of the death
Of the beloved – does the cut earth forgive the worm?

To experience love the wholeness of the heart
Must be split as perfectly as a birch log
And tossed in the fire of poetic cliché.
Thunk. That's all it took! The more
You split a heart the greater it becomes
Until all death is settled in the death of the self
Which can never occur except in a moment of extreme
Self-torture for at the moment of death
There is no moment – only the open heart
Bursting with endless hypocritical laughter.
Natalia was alive and now she is not.
Natalia not? Never! Aye that's the knot.
Fear death? Fear this thought in the mind?
This heap of dumb onions is for death's dominion
And for children catching falling leaves
In wild waves of unforgettable nothingness.

Hark! The kitten is crying again.
It is cold and wet and hungry like everyone.
The one you love is reading these lines.
Giant globs of saltwater are purling down
His or her inevitably adjectival face.

10

October mind in the sky, October
Heart in the earth, the harvest is in
As it always is, and these humiliations
Are porters of the sea and land
Teasing you with hints about your fate
Like the angel lady who lives in your soul
And continually tells you she will never leave
And turns all time into a supermarket
And all space into your own empty stomach.
The earth is a rotten pineapple crawling with
Maggots. Smoke, like streams of strange music,

Rises from all the little houses in the mountains
And destroys forever all your beloved lyricisms
And she looks at you from across the room
And later the room looks at you from across her,
Mountains unmistakably lost forever unlike
Certain mountains in certain books of childhood,
The childhood you see wherever you look.
Oh, her eyes were as buttery as burnt almonds
And the room was continually shifting gears
Like that most wonderful song, "A Sports Car
On a Mountain Road." Something you didn't
Want to sing or drive.
                              Alas, illuminating heavens,
The music rises from these little alpine dwellings
And the little dwellings in all the little centuries.
Her eyes split your heart in twain and burned
Each half black as Plutonian mushrooms.
Her eyes destroyed all understanding
In a solitude of oranges and cherryblossoms
In the rainy English summer of 1594.
Her eyes were inverted nipples flooding
Her brain with constant optical cream. Her eyes
Were dying soldiers in an ancient war.
Her eyes were the hearts of unknown assassins.

But the radiant night has a humour of its own
Which delights in destroying your noblest verse
And farts in your face as you lie dreaming
Of eyes that remind you of the first pair of leaves
On the first branch of the first tree in Eden
And your heart pounding with wild surmise
And her eyes were perfect lovers fated
Never to come together and never part.
Her eyes were planets of negative desire
In a world where poetry and poetry
Can never part and never come together.

11

The human heart delivers itself
In plain brown language,
The language of shameless goddesses,
And gives itself to inexplicably
Erotic monologues so monstrously dull
Newspapers have to be invented
Far from the broken eye of paradise
Frightful in cold feet on a bare night under
Stars as steadfast as neo-Keatsian rhymesters
And the seasons have their seasonings of which
The least intelligent are most knowledgeable.
But the illusion of the heart's loneliness
Is as pitiable as the heart's subtle realization
That it will never be lonely again is glorious,
As the heart unfolds its banner of open sores
Across moonlit landscapes and the first of an entire
Season of falling stars falls softly on its flesh
And pearls pop out like beads of melting chocolate.

12

These words will embarrass me for the rest of my life
By reminding me of my memory's soft spots:
The hungry cat is crying. Reading is dreaming,
Writing is waking up and John Keats is staring
At the face of a dying soldier, purple and green,
In the parking lot of the Banff Springs Hotel,
June afternoon, everyone gone except security guards,
The mountains giant pyramids in the sun,
And Keats points out a long silent freight train
Skirting the base of a mountain away in the distance.
And death's breath carves another line of verse
While the pearl of great price opens like a nose
And squirts you in the face. Seventh Day Adventists

Please read no further. All others please continue.
So there's Keats still complaining about Shelley
And the soldier in the last gasp of his agony
Glimpses a great happiness at the end of a perfect
Language with no grammar but that of the open heart.

The heart is easily bored and loves to read romantic
Novels that will never be written. The heart holds
A hundred-gallon aquarium containing hundreds of tiny
Heartfish nibbling on the green slime of former
Obsessions, and spectacularly respects its assumption
Of emotional imperialism. Friends, the heart is no masochist
Although nothing hurts like a herd of hurt hearts
Or so I've heard. And when day is done and the stars squirt
Ketchup and Hollywood corpses sail across the sky like clouds
The heart becomes insane with incredible life;
Country of terrible sunshine on shipwrecks,
Country of naïve folksingers and generous priestesses
Where the streets run with golden phoenix secretions
And gondoliers regard the earth as a ductless gland,
Language devolving from mysterious inner cavities
Like planetary systems from the sun. And the moon
Bobs in an ocean of dirty dishwater of course.
So simple even a child could put it together.
And what a child hath put together let no god
Prevent the environment from taking on a life
Of its own for we're all in the same wooden horse.
Inevitably, the moon illuminates a charming channel
Where talking cats confound sentimental sailors
With limited intellectual resources by offering
Inexpensive aphrodisiacs. One minute a cat starts talking
Politics and the next you have a dog on your hands.

And blood flows in all directions. Oh look!
A nest full of baby ospreys. And a young photographer
In a long overcoat. Life, I want more and more of you.
Each year I love you more and more.

The burning blackberry stands at the checkout
Counter of time's supermarket and flows in all
Directions. Civilization is more obsessed with beauty
Than a quick look at the twentieth century would indicate
But no more than that elegant young photographer
About to be murdered by loan sharks in the east end
Of Hamilton, Ontario, in 1951. Awake: overcoats
Like that become more and more fashionable
As each generation is born less furry
And with less fury. Asleep: the loss of fur
Necessitates the sort of intelligence capable
Of inventing a long overcoat (the old
Let's-pretend-the-statue-is-alive routine) (the
Open overcoat exposing the music's genitalia).
You need another line here. That'll do.

BARRY McKINNON

SEX AT THIRTY-ONE

for Brian Fawcett & David Phillips

part 1

to leave.   to leave.   beyond that pure (it seems so)
moon.   these gulfs in ourselves, thus ...
to leave with it.   live with each edge
of cloud that takes a ring of light – yet what is
forbidden, that we cannot hold ourselves.
wanting.
as if love, within its
boundaries is another moon.   we walk on it.   talk
until the rain goes.   let what we
want be the whole body of imagination.   released.   hold
me in this light

how we had forgotten, in this awkwardness,
that others exist – discovered a privacy best to be
without.   beyond it, is the
real, yet it requires decision – any pleasure we
seek.   we are this old.   to know.   & speechless,
without sounds, to that extent, a part.   I would wish
you love.   it wouldn't matter, you said, who
it was

I thought the world was
outside & it is.
                  it is not a circus with plastic
ducks to shoot at. some will say it
is coming back to the difficulty of relationships

difficulty. you will go or leave.
I sit most of the time. in the dark of someone's intent, a
relationship forms.

it is so dark, I can barely
see it form

I must invent you. I forget the
greek gods. who will replace them in
this tawdriness

                this timelessness of sex

was it said that ancients, say,
chinese, sat by pools of golden fish
drank wine, enough to
                beckon women with little
                say
                    (I wonder how they saw or spoke of
                    love. but men. they
still do,
              still do fall in pools of
      fish

I thought the smell of clover love.
it was memory (that clear field
                of august.

now the bypass surrounds us, the curve
of memory at 31
                (as if nothing changed

there are no trees left
at the pine centre mall.   I could care
less

for a moment I thought the smell of clover love.

there is nothing to understand

give me an idea of who I am. expect
   something.

the fool in me   is an old lyric – the disembodied
   source I long for

                & more

it is that we go on.

& there is no image
            for it

where are you in this desire
this tension of ...

love is no cup.   can be no more than what
we imagine.   that language in its various ...
(form brings it, yet what is this void – the gulf as some
difficult river, the cessation of an act of form, as love
is an act of the imagination or flesh.   how I go around
the cup or mirror to see in that glance another looking
back, with what intention.   this point of silence and the
clear seed spread on the belly of all women, those I
imagine.   the one, which one follows, beckons.   is this, or she
the goddess, the hag – the one who holds the cup from
which any man could drink or refuse

part 2

try nothing on for size
it fits, that in this world
the heart will give out from pushing volkswagens,

that what we look for, is a joke.   one more hopeless
push, driven to get there – notice how we hardly move
at all

that old sense as I move backward.

they thought I was sick, in love.   to reach 31
& get put to someone elses use.
                                            another
close call to brush against love.   thinking it
an object, the garbage man took my art.   there was
nothing else
I could do with it

increasing amount smoked.   another way to measure
distance.   in this fog, my moon has disappeared.   I will
draw more easily the moon forth, than you, who ever
you are, my aphrodite, my earth, my
butterfly

what was it I was to say.   these years pass
without a moment

so I return to what was simple & intended, had no
more to do with any thing

than a hand & flesh.   some kiss, stolen I thought

what humans do in this other
difficulty.   despite it

the head swirl's look.   I go thru the drawers
for language & know I won't find it, or you
as hidden as I.

but we did speak.   I think it was dawn, & I
couldn't sleep for thought of infidelity

to discover in you   what is in me

we haven't spoken
since

I forego desire.   I forego the flesh, so
caught in my own I resist
the others.   we are so ... I bought a record.
I bought you a lock.   who shares the combinations,
who opens the heart & what is said.   jealousy is as desire.   do
we seek, or love, or ... what is, this that is
hidden & how to reveal
it

sex at 31.   men so lost in talk they will not
see her.   I must look in the dictionary
to find aphrodite.   look again to wives who
inhabit these kitchens, cursed by what
they think they are – the bodies drawn, or fat.
I will hold you.   I will wash
these dishes.   heat up this food

but where did you go

take men as
the early going moon.   imagine us
at 31 more in love than what we thought could
be.

bpNICHOL

INCHOATE ROAD

I

1
in Choate Road
a car stalled
underneath the bridge i
pass over
another fragment

water spill
the frozen spume of
the river
     runs thru Port Hope
into

winter storm across the lake's imperfect ice
blue gaps in the clouds & snow
older worlder order
o der wrld er wrl o
inchoate world

2
life like lake like
    line
      lingers
a dream of
ocean and
pacific one i was born by
bounded in that first family
superior as the other shore
crossing the land bridge between
ocean-going vessels steaming into
both ports i
was there
    sea to sea

all i needed was
to let the water take me
home

3
i was taught it as
their history
                    but it made sense:

1 if by land
                    (you can make it on foot)
2 if by sea
                    (i need
a boat
            to carry me
                        OUT
                                THERE

4
water music

two rivers
winding thru

Winnipeg

ocean & lake

what our music
                    our poems come
down to
            the sea in

"everything gives way &
nothing stays fixed"

"the river shines
between the villages"

two translations

see how they wind
this way & that

this name or
another

    tracking me

5
"for other waters are
continually flowing on"

       & other songs

emptying out

spring into stream into river into lake into
ocean
   'n ocean 'n
      ocean
       'n ocean 'n
         ocean
           'n ocean 'n
             ocean

6
in Choate Road
the cars go by
exhaust blue
late january frost

i thot the water spill
a broken mill
going too fast &
couldn't quite connect it

the image

& beyond that
the town &
beyond that the lake &
beyond that

7
this is the world

not these words

not this poem

this is the world

II

1
snow out the window's light
glimmer's outline
ships, a bay
(anchored)

across this page
a light moves
in the water's now
wet blackness of the street
empty stretches snowy beach
reach as far as i can see into the darkness around this bay

window'd prairie sky
empty hole dug
makes a pond the city will not let them put water in &
then the tree 'n trees
mark the twisting course of

these lines stretch across a country   a life   snow falls   birds &
i grow older with every word
every liquid gesture flows from this blue pen   watermarks
mark time
my life by
the side of
this bodies these

2
beginning with lead & wood
mark the course of this writing's later
ink as the words begin to flow

late   rink lights coming on
shouts of the kids on the frozen water &
later   th'aw
flooding spring
hot stretches of summer
falls
        ice/water
        ice/water
        ice

3
pigeons on the track, a rack
ing cough ing
breath's frozen face

mouth of the assiniboine/red
(river)(brick)(engine of the train)
under the bridge the birds
nest along the top ledge of
abandoned factory across the river to
St Boni face to face
with memory at the mere's edge
more'n merely water goes
one into the other
                              (seen from the plane) those
alphabets these
rivers
            strokes of
pens together in the plain
words   dried ink   dyes
strained thru   books
the stain of thinking
the rivers the
type we were
down at the mouth
where the two come together
watching our breath
lines of trees
track across the river tracks we was
thinking of writing
vast expanse of white twisting no

4
not so much that but this

not so much then but now

not so much beginnings but beginning

again's a gain

a river arrive
air ver-y cold &

the drift

under the stillness
the silent stretches
a current accrues
air collide us

not so much the river but the riven
moment (more meant to you than

then this

5
out window the light
damned width of the river's length
twists thru the mountains
clouds   just below the tops
twist too the two
wind thru &
                  the river's
ever varied very song the
birds & the snow & the
very hush of the damned world goes
dawn & on   ocean   river
               lake   stream

i was in river

i was lost in lake

i was caught in the twist &
toss in the water

                        (essential's pull
                        these pools
                        perception
falls

all's a damn now
a pulsated
full)

o
  'n tary
o
  'n hurry
o
  'n linger

    (so that these rhythms are established
    closure (details – what we call a
    theme) globular, returning, the
    circumnavigation of
    the work/world
o)

  'cean 'n stay
o
  'n go
o-ke-an-o
winds thru the poem the
words say slower & slower the
eaupen measure of

(i stood at the edge of o & e

a u (au – "to") the translation where

e goes in these
l'eau countries

6
in the snow world
slowed wheels rumble
the heaped flow of the crystals grow
around us
white's white shift
slips thru the hung trees
line the slopes of these mountain valleys &
we drift on as the snow mounts
higher climbing
towards an imagined top or ridge
entrances the cloud world hid
to the fall now
thru snow, white clouds
the world be/l'eau

7
o eau (eaucean)

o world (lake
river, path the vowels take
to the sea)

eau io
i 'nvoke you
sometimes

        why?

o beginning gaining
vision of the water
births you int'

o

      wave of speech
sound sine g

s-ing
     ing
            mouther
sonne
         farther

INK o it
!*whirl*!

8
giggle mesh

looking for the place the puns flesh out
the body of speech is
re vealed, the veil
drops away
the dance!
sheer ecstasy of glimmering
part icles part airy
nothingnessence
flow of grammar hammers in
my chest, the breath's pressed OUT
quick liquid spout of
the wail:
THOT
        a kind of harbour or
land
and m and no
places the eyes rest
flat/calm/march/day
– still snow still –
(did i expect it to blow away?)

pair of dice
-adox
pay the price &
get your change

"do you have exact change?"
i can only approximate

vapour

how the words (the selves) twist
every chance you take

water
watair

                (dew

                          dawn
                deer on the lawn below me
                river rushes &
                clouds &

                          (water rodes
                          the passes: the
                          rocks & twists of
                          river bubbling up from
                          earth falling
                          emptying out (somewhere)
                          beyond

                                                water

int'
          a i 'r
o

III

river riven

wandering the length up & down
when was it i

---

        quoted myself
        into the world

I
word'l get you world

flood of feeling

when the river
overflows its banks
mudder
        no fodder now

floating away in a boat from the house
Winnipeg 1950
that fall we nailed a donkey to the wall
just below the window on the second floor
to mark how high the water'd risen

flood was the word i learned
& rain & river, water
drove me out of my world
mother/father
into another

2
ech-

eau

vo-cab-u-lar-y
diction airy or
at best suspect

flood

mud

(wreck

row)

two rivers known
two more as the summer comes & goes

Red Assiniboine
Saskatchewan Bow

wryme

old wyrm
ouroboros

i-row-ny
(set out in a pun t'
cross this
sudden sea)

3
the trick is to know the depth always
& that the surface'll get you there

the flood'll bring the bottom to the top

spins & the spinner marks the spot
the line drops down

the hook's only visible when
you get more than your feet wet

4
rhy-
wry thm
    theme

two in-
separable
tune

leer ich
(sneer "i")

trance forms
within you (around you)

dusk rain on the harbourfront
from the café chair
gulls gulled
i am engulfed, flooded with
même mer, 'e says, or
the same more 'e
experienced be-
fore

feelings flow
like a river
the river flowed
like a river at flood tide
watch the lake rise
rainy august night
or maybe ordinary
like a jewel eye
glittering in a real face
sudden surprise of the place
the distraction of resemblances

– in land sea
– under ground river
– fire water
– air stream

wa of birth
    of water
       waltz

wan
      (one

           (singular ich's istence))

                    along a rain-pocked river
                    across this rain-pocked lake

sea
be { gan
    gins

a   gain

      air ' rain
     'n a trance later

two in one
wanders the flood
plain

5
among the bushes
the brush the
rushes the
different rivers i followed the courses of
– Assiniboine, Red, Seine, Neebing, McIntyre, Kaministiqua –
some i knew the proper names of
we called them all "the river"

    heading upstream
    tracking the beaver dams
    flooded bush
    collecting bullrushes for
    my mother   fell
    full face in the mud

    slow meander of sludge brown water swam in
    shit drifting by
    sewage from the towns lay south of us

learned those names for water
(sky aspect – storm –
intermixed with elemental fire
the sign for "loud noise")
understood the local & the univeral
but moved too often to make the local my own

i was born from water
bore me away from home
again & again after i was born

6
"i should've been a sailor"

wasn't

7
the contradiction is
to spend your life on land
trance fixed in
the sea

contra the diction is
the land wage
(when the water comes
– sea pun – you pay a
price)
            pays

                flood

                flawed

                flowed

                        (how you move from
                        imperfection to imperfection in
                        the world)

my body is water
my life is water
                ich
            eau ech
            eau
            eau

8
ink eau
ate world

our obra is
the water works
hydro eclectic

tide ties me in this flux
the surface   change is
constantly

when the flood resided
i saw we'd lived
under the sea
all those years

i never saw it til
water covered me
clouds blew by
sea 'n
folds of fields appeared in air
i saw the saints there
& here &

i think in ink
particle charged airs
hum
            anity
      in
            anity
            an ity world a
pen opens
floods over me

i write from the bottom of a see
step out upon the surface

poetic feet give me access to
stare cases
& where that leads me
floods the white plain page is
ground/sea/sky

            inchoate world
                words

seaquence

      "the way", we say,
      "the letters lie"

Epilogue

35,000 feet above Saskatchewan
less than a foot between me &
all that air, these airs err
insubstantial as comparison
spots to which we come, position ourselves
heirs to the veaucabulairies
terrer that fires us
all gollems finally
someone marks our foreheads
four elements there
                we lurch forward
enact tradition
           monstrously
familiair
        familheir
tri bull
        labyrinthinemine
a tour of
gnossos
logos

osos
        (o that s.o.s. of
consciousgnoss)

or that old question
"who's the boss?" (b.s. os)

minos most of our memory
we function out of loss
amigos

            unless i've got a pun
i can't write it down

ink think

"is that what you mean by procoss?"
(harbour lights
th'arbor of masts &
sails off the edge of your world   a view
venue   sTREEtS
lower&upper
middle voice/tongue/world)
i mean the earthyear the puns get the more the pen can pin it down to

Pan plays the world 'pon his flute

old bullfoot amazes us
pipes bright as language

                    sleepy giants

who will wake you
mourn your death &
dance your resurrection

                    dreaming world

(the rivers branch like
trees
                    someone's always leaving

(catch in the voice the
ship

                    water water water you
                    doing?

(meme eau: i'm just looking at the sea 'n world

                                        (eauver & eauver)))
something fishy when the tongue slips

(glimmering surface
invisible depths
across which the boats skip)

"I'll write you a letter"
(A to A))

giant talk

the long waged war
the fight or struggle for
the mind
          boarders in these rooms words open

i said that be

you said that be   }   FORE

we said that be

they said that be

warned

letting the future know
we're playing thru
gulf the gulls & mist rise out of
stretches between "me" & "you"

MICHAEL ONDAATJE

TIN ROOF

She hesitated. "Are you being romantic now?"
"I'm trying to tell you how I feel without exposing myself. You know what I mean?"

Elmore Leonard

*

You stand still for three days
for a piece of wisdom
and everything falls to the right place

or wrong place

                    You speak
            don't know whether
seraph or bitch
flutters at your heart

and look through windows
for cue cards
blazing in the sky.
                    The solution.
This last year I was sure
I was going to die

*

The geography of this room   I know so well
tonight   I could rise in the dark
sit at the table   and write without light.
I am here in the country of warm rains.
A small cabin – a glass, wood,
tin bucket on the Pacific Rim.

            Geckoes climb
the window to peer in,
and all day the tirade pale blue waves
touch the black shore of volcanic rock

and fall to pieces here

*

How to arrive at this
drowning
on the edge of sea

      (How to drive
the Hana Road, he said –
one hand on the beer
one hand on your thigh
and one eye for the road)

Waves leap to this cliff all day
and in the evening lose
their pale blue

he rises from the bed
as wind from three directions
falls, takes his place
on the peninsula of sheets
which also loses colour

stands in the loose green kimono
by a large window and gazes

through gecko
past the deadfall
into sea,

      the unknown magic he loves
throws himself into

          the blue heart

*

Tell me
all you know
about bamboo

growing wild, green
growing up into soft arches
in the temple ground

the traditions

driven through hands
through the heart
during torture

and most of all

                this

small bamboo pipe
not quite horizontal
that drips
every ten seconds
to a shallow bowl

I love this
being here
not a word
just the faint
fall of liquid
the boom of an iron buddhist bell
in the heart rapid
as ceremonial bamboo

*

To be lost

A man buying wine
Rainier beer at the store
would he be satisfied with this?
Cold showers, electric skillet,
Red River on TV
Oh he could be

(Do you want
            to be happy and write?)

He happens to love the stark
luxury of this place
– no armchairs, a fridge of beer and mangoes

        Precipitation.

To avoid a story   The refusal to move

All our narratives of sleep
a mild rumble to those inland

            Illicit pockets of
            the kimono

Heart like a sleeve

*

The cabin
            its tin roof
a wind run radio
catches the noise of the world.
He focuses on the gecko
almost transparent body
how he feels now
everything passing through him like light.
In certain mirrors
he cannot see himself at all.
He is joyous and breaking down.
The tug over the cliff.
What protects him
is the warmth in the sleeve

that is all, really

*

We go to the stark places of the earth
and find moral questions everywhere

Will John Wayne and Montgomery Clift
take their cattle to Missouri or Kansas?

Tonight I lean over the Pacific
and its blue wild silk
ringed by creatures
who
    tchick tchick tchick
my sudden movement
who say nothing else.

There are those who are in
and there are those who look in

Tiny leather toes
hug the glass

*

On the porch
thin ceramic
chimes
          ride wind
off the Pacific

bells of the sea

          I do not know
the name of large orange flowers
which thrive on salt air
lean half drunk
against the steps

Untidy banana trees
thick moss on the cliff
and then the plunge
to black volcanic shore

It is impossible to enter the sea here
except in a violent way

          How we have moved
from thin ceramic

to such destruction

*

All night
          the touch

of wave on volcano.

There was the woman
who clutched my hair
like a shaken child.
The radio whistles
round a lost wave length.

All night slack-key music
and the bird whistling *duino*
duino, words and music
entangled in pebble
ocean static.
The wild sea and her civilization
the League of the Divine Wind
and traditions of death.

          Remember
those women in movies
who wept into the hair
of their dead men?

*

Going up stairs
I hang my shirt
on the stiff
ear of an antelope

Above the bed
            memory
restless green bamboo
            the distant army
assembles wooden spears

her feet braced
on the ceiling
sea in the eye

Reading the article
an 1825 report   *Physiologie du Gout*
on the artificial growing of truffles
speaks
            of "vain efforts
and deceitful promises,"
commandments of culinary art

Good
morning to your body
hello nipple
and appendix scar like a letter
of too much passion
from a mad Mexican doctor

All this noise at your neck!

heart clapping

like green bamboo

        this earring
     which
has flipped over
    and falls
        into the pool of your ear

The waves against black stone
that was a thousand year old
burning red river
could not reach us

*

Cabin

"hana"

      this *flower* of wood
in which we rose
out of the blue sheets
you thin as horizon
reaching for lamp or book
my shirt

      hungry
for everything about the other

here we steal places to stay
as we steal time
      never too proud to beg,
even if we never
see the other's grin and star again

there is nothing resigned
in this briefness
we swallow complete

I will know everything here

      this cup
          balanced on my chest
      my eye witnessing the petal
      drop away from its order,
      your arm

for ever

precarious in all our fury

*

Every place has its own wisdom. Come.
Time we talked about the sea,
the long waves
                    "trapped around islands"

*

There are maps now whose portraits
have nothing to do with surface

Remember the angels, floating compasses
– Portolan atlases so complex
we looked down and never knew
which was earth which was sea?
The way birds the colour of prairie
confused by the sky
flew into the earth
(Remember those women
who claimed dead miners
the colour of the coal they drowned in)

The bathymetric maps startle.
Visions of the ocean floor
troughs, naked blue deserts,
Ganges Cone, the Mascarene Basin

so one is able now
in ideal situations
to plot a stroll
to new continents
"doing the Berryman walk"

And beneath the sea
there are
these giant scratches
of pain
the markings of
some perfect animal
who has descended
burying itself

under the glossy
ballroom

or they have to do with ascending,
what we were, the earth creatures
longing for horizon.
I know one thing
our sure non-sliding
civilized feet
our small leather shoes
did not make them

(Ah you should be happy and write)

I want the passion
which puts your feet on the ceiling
this fist
to smash forward

take this silk
            somehow   *Ah*
out of the rooms of poetry

(Listen, solitude, X wrote,
  is not an absolute,
  it is just a resting place)

listen   in the end
the pivot from angel to witch
depends on small things
this animal, the question
are you happy?

No I am not happy

lucky though

*

Rainy Night Talk

Here's to
the overlooked
nipples of Spain
            brown Madrid areolae
kneecaps of Ohio girls
kneeling in the palms of men
waiting to be thrown high
into the clouds
of a football stadium

        Here's to
the long legged
woman from Kansas
whispering good morning at 5,
        dazed
in balcony moonlight

All that drizzle the night before
walking walking through rain
slam her car door
and wrote my hunger out, the balcony
like an entrance
to a city of suicides.

Here's to the long legs
driving home
in more and more rain
weaving like a one-sided
lonely conversation
over the mountains

And what were you
carrying? in your head
that night Miss
Souri? Miss Kansas?

while I put my hands
sweating
on the cold
window
on the edge
of the trough of this city?

*

Breaking down after logical rules
couldn't be the hit and run driver
I wanted Frank Sinatra
I was thinking blue pyjamas
I was brought up on movies and song!

I could write my suite of poems
for Bogart   drunk
six months after the departure at Casablanca.
I see him lying under the fan
at the Slavyansky Bazar Hotel
and soon he will see the truth
the stupidity of his gesture
he'll see it in the space
between the whirling metal.

                    Stupid fucker
he says to himself, stupid fucker
and knocks the bottle
leaning against his bare stomach
onto the sheet. Gin stems
out like a four leaf clover.
I used to be lucky he says
I had white suits black friends
who played the piano ...
                    and that
was a movie I saw just once.

What about Burt Lancaster
limping away at the end of *Trapeze?*
Born in 1943. And I saw that six times.

(I grew up knowing I could never fly)

That's me. You. Educated
at the *Bijou*. And don't ask me
about my interpretation of "Madame George."
That's a nine minute song
a two hour story.

So how do we discuss
the education of our children?
Teach them to be romantics
to veer towards the sentimental?
Toss them into the air like Tony Curtis
and make 'em do the triple somersault
through all these complexities
and commandments?

*

Oh Rilke, I want to sit down calm like you
or pace the castle, avoiding the path of the cook, Carlo,
who believes down to his turnip soup
that you speak the voice of the devil.
I want the long lines my friend spoke of
that bamboo which sways muttering
like wooden teeth in the slim volume I have
with its childlike drawing of Duino Castle.
I have circled your book for years
like a wave combing
the green hair of the sea
kept it with me, your name
a password in the alley.
I always wanted poetry to be that
but this solitude brings no wisdom
just two day old food in the fridge,
certain habits you would not approve of.
If I said all of your name now
it would be the movement
of the tide you soared over
so your private angel
could become part of a map.

I am too often busy with things
I wish to get away from, and I want
the line to move slowly now, slow
-ly like a careful drunk across the street
no cars in the vicinity
but in his fearful imagination.
How can I link your flowing name
to geckoes or a slice of octopus?
Though there are Rainier beer cans,
magically, on the windowsill.

And still your lovely letters
January 1912 near Trieste.
The car you were driven in
"at a snail's pace"
through Provence. Wanting
"to go into chrysalis ...
to live by the heart and nothing else."
Or your guilt –

                "I howl at the moon
                with all my heart
                and put the blame
                on the dogs"

I can see you sitting down
the suspicious cook asleep
so it is just you
and the machinery of the night
that foul beast that sucks and drains
leaping over us sweeping our determination
away with its tail. Us and the coffee,
all the small charms we invade it with.

As at midnight we remember the colour
of the dogwood flower growing
like a woman's sex outside the window.
I wanted poetry to be walnuts
in their green cases
but now it is the sea
and we let it drown us,
and we fly to it released
by giant catapults
of pain loneliness deceit and vanity

LOLA LEMIRE
TOSTEVIN
GYNO-TEXT

for my children

a
different
tongue
to
pen
a
trait

le
trait
d'union

hymen
hyphens
gender

two
constrictions
made
one

where
orifice
fills
function

pulsation
gives
&
takes

V
notch
of I
dentity

a
legend
at
leg's
end

through
the
cervix
the
helix
leaks
a
dream

Out of O
into
the
narrow
bare
but
for
this
foreign
marrow

nucleus
cleaves
until
all
that's
left
is
cleft

sound
of
soft
solder

flash
of
flesh
weld

pregnant
pause
as
conceptual
space

interval
between
inner
outer
folds

sens
et
sang
prennent
corps

prêtent
l'oreille
au
texte
qui
s'organise

fluttering
flinch
inch
by
inch
into
invisible
vise

oral
pit
spits
yolk
spins
spine

embryo
rolled
in
a
scroll

dismembered
shape
in
soluble
space
so
splendidly
suspended

ridge
gives
rise
to
gut
tied
tongue

tugs
the
lingual
hinge

l'épique
impose
tandis
que
l'épine
n'est
qu'un
épisode
dorsal

thick
trunk
unleashes
leaf
limb

bud
tender
lotus

voice
boxed
in
ears
echo
deeper
pounding
tympa
tym
    panic
rhythm
of a
heart
some
w)here

eye
ball O
n stalk
sucks
brain

flows
Over
lid
fOld

wisp
of
rib

body's
first
articulations
broach
bone
by
bone

first
thump

the
throb
that
throttles

le
point
d'exclamation
est
la
mise
au
point
névralgique

uterine
tattoo
your
indelible
code
tapped
against
your
small
cell
wall

&
belly
bells
in
abdominal
dome

wells
inside
out

cordon
rond
dit
ronronnement

arrondit
le
ventre
au
verbe

opened
furrow
shows
its
sex
translated

palate
joined

heart
hollow
divides
two
ounces
of
bloody
love
&
bitter
ness

taste
buds
trickle
salt
in
fine
hair
filament

lanugo
hairs
lunula
nails

ten
half
moons
struck

synaptic
reflex
skips
a
syllable

triggers
flesh
flèche
to
the
target

papillae

alar
lamina
wings
the
lateral
wall

vena
cava
excavates

runs
its
ruts
&
turns

skin
skims
the
surface

the
swallow
in
skull's
hollow

cochlea
cocks
an
ear
to
tides
whorls
&
sinews

brain
blooms
white
webs
hemmed
in
spheres
hung
loose
ly

dark
areolae
circle
nipples
black
raw
nib

in
silk
milk

mute
skeleton
moves
to
muscle
string
pulled
taut
from
A
to
Zone

vagin
vagir
enfin

FRED WAH

THIS DENDRITE MAP: FATHER/ MOTHER HAIBUN

Father / Mother Haibun #1

Finally changed the calendar today to August. Sitting here this morning trying to figure out things (phone rings and she asks "Is this David? I must have the wrong number. I don't know why I keep doing this.") the *ecrit* I'm open for, ungular, now alone in the mornings looking through Jung and Hillman for hints, I mean the simple and solid clarity of my father's father's dying, his dying, and then me living and then dying too is outrageous, bald as geographical Saskatchewan and my Grandfather which made my life "racial" not that he actually came to be there but simply him here/there and her, my Grandmother, her Salvation Army Englishness really solid in the middle of his flux but both of them cutting "geo" out of their world thus Maple Creek Moose Jaw North Battleford Medicine Hat somewhere in England and Canton China places in their lives much more than in their world, you, my father, almost too, thus me, such particles caught in the twig-jam holding the water back impedimenta and this dendrite map I'm finally on now for no reason but time, and then I'll go to the city and look for an S-shaped chair to hold me and this up.

Two weeks late I turn the calendar, crave for ripe tomatoes

Father / Mother Haibun #2

Anger the same thing as you behind my face, eyes, maybe. A larger than usual black bear, eating, high up in the thin wild cherry trees in the gulley this morning, sun just coming up. I peer around the corner of the garage at the bear just like you would, eyes squinted brow lined in suspicion like yours used to, as if you were trying to figure out something serious. I feel your face in me like that sometimes, looking out of me, and now I wonder if my anger is the same as yours flying out of me from him and his, etc. the anger molten back through Chthonic fear. The bear flushed off, finally, by the dog. You hover in the cool August morning air, behind my eyes. The fire, the candle, the pumpkin, the "virtu," inside.

Crash of broken branch, hungry, pits in the shit

Father / Mother Haibun #3

I try talking to you in this near-September air after I water the dry spots
out of the lawn, morning sunny and clear the air coming to this for
months ahead, almost, your death-month, turning the flowers, even
those huckleberries I picked yesterday had thoughts of the frost ahead
high in the mountains, such simple weather but something more
primitive here pictures of the kids each year on the first day of school in
front of the flowers in their new clothes, ahead, you too and my mind
working over the connections, you're laughing, sceptical, like when I
told you they used hot water to make the ice at the arena because it
steams and you just about believed it because I did, my heart shoots into
the memory of that actual mouths-and-eyes-talking dialogue, weather is
memory every time I wonder if you ever really listened to the songs on
the Wurlitzer in the cafe, particularly on a quiet winter Sunday
afternoon, the words anytime your mind roaming ahead and behind like
mine the little shots at living each day all the things air
carries for thinking like that.

**Music, I try to think of the words to Autumn Leaves, Love
Letters in the Sand**

Father / Mother Haibun #4

Your pen wrote Chinese and your name in a smooth swoop with flourish and style, I can hardly read my own tight scrawl, could you write anything else, I know you could read, nose in the air and lick your finger to turn the large newspaper page pensively in the last seat of those half-circle arborite counters in the Diamond Grill, your glass case bulging your shirt pocket with that expensive pen, always a favourite thing to handle the way you treated it like jewelry, actually it was a matched pen and pencil set, Shaeffer maybe (something to do with Calgary here), heavy, silver, black, gold nib, the precision I wanted also in things, that time I conned you into paying for a fountain pen I had my eye on in Benwell's stationery store four dollars and twenty cents Mom was mad but you understood such desires in your cheeks relaxed when you worked signing checks and doing the books in the back room of the cafe late at night or how the pen worked perfectly with your quick body as you'd flourish off a check during a busy noon-hour rush the sun and noise of the town and the cafe flashing.

High muck-a-muck's gold-toothed clicks ink mark red green
on lottery blotting paper, 8-spot (click, click)

Father / Mother Haibun #5

You can't drive through a rainbow I said hills to myself in the mountains
glory of a late summer early fall thunder storm the Brilliant Bluffs
brilliant indeed the shine rain and sunshine waves of science breaking
lickety split school systems memory for the next word after colour from
the other side no one could see it otherwise nature's path is home to the
bluebird triangular son/event/father w/ time-space China rainbow over
your youth vertical like on the prairies that rainbow stood straight up
into the sky on the horizon you'd think in the winter sun ice crystals
could form unbelievable

**Radio on, up north an American hunter shoots a rare
white moose, geese in the sky, nibbling ribbons**

Father / Mother Haibun #6

I wish you were alive here in my life so we could share the ease of our lives growing older together, now time would catch up with the gap of our ages, 45-72, ethnicity would be gone, just skin and the winding down, the fence Jenefer & I built along the back, hockey games, the sunny fall day, this sentimentalism, songs too, like crazy white American juke box "Mule Train" in your imagination I thought just as those events are in mine, no, but you and the Great Lakes boats desire, absolutely your own, undying care for the single, your own world fact, all this buffer, as down the road in the village from us this so-called community, the ones we care for really spread over the whole earth if possible, padding of the family too, this softness around ourselves so that we want it, so common we could talk about it now, but so alone, so alone.

**I'll stain the fence red, a dim border in the snow, might
last thirty years**

Father / Mother Haibun #7

I was back in Buffalo when you died and when I came out for your
funeral at the end of September there was snow on Elephant Mountain
as far down as Pulpit Rock from Ernie's house the lake quiet my mother
alone suddenly, months unused, unusual, I knew you best in the winter
when there was curling and hockey or in the summer when we fished,
dark mornings on the way to work or wet leaves in the gutter, driving at
this time of year from Cranbrook to Nelson for the Lion's dance, car
heater toasty warm upholstery, outside the air wet and cool mist hackles
in the mountains your life simply closing down in the quiet month on
the Hume Hotel ballroom floor wobble of the planet's sun seasons
shortened golden flower's corny harvest elixir completed.

Road's nearly empty, only a few pickups with firewood

Father / Mother Haibun #8

The pulse. So. When I take it now the microsystem wild card is almost cellular in its transport of the image imprint forward or I think back pictures. Some Saturday afternoons I'd have to take off work at the Diamond to play soccer down at the Civic, or you'd feed me a steak before a midget hockey bus trip to Trail, after the game Frenchie's french fries outside the Cominco, my earth my world which grosses more sensation, you knew more than I did, now my daughter has grown up into her stomach too, large encryptic sublease a full-grown symptom of I'm just curious about this body. You read it all, playing games is really not such a big deal but I always thought I had to pad it a bit to get off work, the world and out the door down the street, you knew it and me, outside the sun and the chemicals it's either numbers or that large front swinging wooden door.

Felled tree in the fall, I look at the stump for sap, zero

Father / Mother Haibun #9

"Why do you think of your father so much?"

"He's dead. Every once in a while I think I see him, or someone I see reminds me of him, or I'm writing this book and he's in it."

"That's not the truth. There's more to it than that."

"What we'll try for is a paradigm in this."

"You can think of a fishing cause. For him environment is connected with the earth."

"Dante phoned last night. From Salmo. And the day before, Mike Zoll showed up and told me 'The subtle quality of things transcends all formal boundaries.' I don't know, I'm not sure, maybe."

"Do women think a circle is a labyrinth?"

"Kore, no one wears purple like you. I half expect you to come with a hat."

"I feel I'm lucky I'm part Chinese when I see a river."

"So. What about your father?"

"Look, it's an old problem. When Smaro says 'Alley Alley Home Free' I know exactly what's going on. Her eyes twinkle. Here, it's snowing today. Sounds are deadened, like waking up in a room with the windows closed. Why do you ask?"

"'Autumn in New York,' 'Moonlight in Vermont,' they're all haiku. And that's just one of the tricks Lionel knows. You know that poem about his dad and the echo of the axe on the other side of the valley? That was in the fall, there was frost. Or Victor's poem, 'Kenkyusha: Day Nine,' his daughter's birth, my father's death, zooming in on the phoneme of time, accurate, and asks me 'what time.'"

"You'd better ask Peter about Jack Clarke's Hegel's 'discipline of service and obedience' and 'the lake Fred Wah said it all ends up in' in case McNaughton and the hidden 'd' can help."

"Maybe tomorrow. I've been carrying it around all week. It's the epitaph to my Aunt Hannah's grave in Swift Current. It's like a song. Whenever I think of it I can hear my Granny Wah singing, front row, in the Salvation Army hall, and I can see her grey-blue eyes softened with a bit of surprise."

Hannah Elizabeth

fell asleep in Jesus Arms

1918-1936

Father / Mother Haibun #10

Working with my back to the window for more natural light, dog chasing cows in the field, the words stubble today, embedded there in the bracken at the edge of the field, Chinese philosophy and numbers, the cloud-filled night, "and they swam and they swam, right over the dam," etc., all this, and sugar too, holding the hook, time, the bag, the book, the shape, you also carried on your back yin and embraced yang with your arms and shoulders, the mind as a polished mirror, there, back into my hand.

**I can't stop looking at the field of brown grass and weed
and feeling the grey sky**

Father / Mother Haibun #11

Mother somewhere you flying over me with love and close careless caress from Sweden your soft smooth creme skin only thoughts from your mother without comparison the lightness of your life/blood womanness which is mine despite language across foetalness what gods of northern europe bring out of this sentence we say and live in outside of the wife of the storm god's frictive battle with the "story" our names

Rain washes first snow, old words here on the notepad,
"Where did Odysseus go?"

Father / Mother Haibun #12

Mom you'll know this as a wordgame, strategy to get truth's attention, your name, Corrine, for example, core, cortex, heart, blood, islands of the liver, a tension to incite the present, your friend Woody written into the texture, coloured uphill under their apple tree beautiful also, we were about fifteen when Wayne Waters said to me "Your mother's a good looking woman" and I blushed, tissue of skin, shades of other people's hair, touch.

The landscape is red, "pudeur," an air of sanctity and respect, etc.

Father / Mother Haibun #13

The issue is to divide into two, duplicate, derive language which is a filter for the blood, and then to replenish thought in a precise flow to converge again on life, how much a copy of you I am also a material for my own initials (F.J.) Karen Marie Erickson when your mother died all the undoubling condensed memory added up to a single snowy winter month like January.

I get up and look, no sky today, just the fog. How one can one be?

Father / Mother Haibun #14

When my hands, arms, and head grew larger there was at one point a
very comforting sensation which I thought might relate to my birth and
you're constantly rubbing your wrist joints this spherical map of
"influence" as in Dad's anger, maybe, or your clearing your throat. I wait
for simply old age and a mental space serrated description narrative the
same refrain female song a flair for the fictive or theory that there is
invocation in the inheritance of the blue-print.

**In winter ravens look more majestic, weaving over the
highway, tree to tree, tree to tree**

Father / Mother Haibun #15

All this imaging is only the subliminal daily cache because of your first
real house and the "Just Mary" show *time* with you in the radio air of
the room carpet *Journeys Through Bookland* "Tom and the Waterbabies"
with story every morning and on Sunday afternoons got "serial" eyes
with "Jake and the Kid" or John Drainey's story hour quiet spring
evenings Sgt. Drake on the Vancouver waterfront breathing radio world
innuendo a mother with secrets when the snow blows in circles over the
farms final connections to the ancient world.

**Someday I'll grow them, prairie hollyhocks again, on a
stucco wall**

Father / Mother Haibun #16

I know the language just turns you into metaphor, rock of ages like Granny Wah, the truth. Traces of the other mothers, cliff-dwellers in the golden city, your windows nothingnesses to the world's something, bisons on the walls at Lascaux. So there. How to defend you and I from a language edited by Christians I stand facing west with my father and speak words which are new names for the sea.

**Old month's countenance, deer swim the rock-wall river,
mean anything to you?**

Father / Mother Haibun #17

Oh Mother, the brightness of the birch tree's bark in this November mid-afternoon sunset, fringes, the datum which is permanent, the external events of all that stuff actual energy is created from, you on a different planar syntax Jenefer discovers in turning the yin/yang key, a cyclic thing going on there, ontologic principle, all the daughters want it, one pot, this morning I watered your Christmas cactus bursting brilliant pink and purple on schedule for your birthday again, and you should see Helen's, what'd those philosophers say, he beats the drum, he stops, he sobs, he sings, they had mothers.

You flew over me, outside there was a moist loss, now I remember

Father / Mother Haibun #18

I'd say that's a "proud" or swollen wound on my finger, body's pride reminding itself of itself, something genitive about the blue sloped roof of the '51 Pontiac, lives broken into car eras both of you (thus us) the heat on the edge of healing skin red something eucharistical and my own two daughters even this spring, fall leeched ground and then outside the flowers see how hard it is for me to make sense of a hunch, looking around myself, looking for the simple "of" connection might be, and why my friend Albert set out his amaryllis this spring.

**No more snow to shovel this winter, back to the ground,
flowers**

Father / Mother Haibun #19

I'm here alone for the weekend, get fires going and burn all that junk, mind keeps that there to clean up. I get some rice on and the cabin's warm. Now I sit here sip a beer and dwell on my aloneness, the solitary singleness and being older now. That is a prediction I gave myself when I watched some of the old men around town, isolation. Night falling. Cold over the lake, fingers of clouds in the western sky above Woodbury Creek. I told Peter that's the process I'm interested in as long as I can keep getting the language out. Now I'm as old as you were. The fire outside in the dark comes from your eyes. The words of our name settle down with everything else on this shore.

Smoke sits on the lake, frost tonight, eyes thinking

Father / Mother Haibun #20

I still don't know how to use the chopsticks as right or as natural, bamboo fingers hands arms mind stomach, food steaming off the dishes, rain or wet snow, windows, night lights, small meals you'd grab between rushes (unlike me), that's what you did, isn't it, went back to the cafe later, on the nights we didn't have rice at home, me too, when I first went to university in Vancouver I couldn't stand it, I'd need rice, catch the Hastings bus to Chinatown, what is it, this food business, this hovering over ourselves?

A little ginger, a little garlic, black beans, lo bok, Aunty Ethel, the kitchen

Father / Mother Haibun #21

Speedy dancing and the leaves of Germany meet me at the elevator, words mean everything, I try to phone you on mother's day, everyone does, more Swedish than Chinese, you didn't want me to be a boy scout all my life, did you (the leaves cling to this writing), sometimes to be battle-ready Norbert Ruebsaat, genetics and geographies, he can tell you too, exactly like mother alphabet the new lyric feet, McKinnon's South America eyesight I tell myself my self-perception, palace/place/police, spring leafless trees on Ontario's horizon, did Pindar catch us dead in our tracks?

**Japanese plum blossoms, my finger joints swollen, your
kind of love sweetest, get that, sweetest**

PHYLLIS WEBB
NAKED POEMS

star fish

fish star

Suite I

MOVING
to establish distance
between our houses.

It seems
I welcome you in.

Your mouth blesses me
all over.

There is room.

AND
here
and here and
here
and over   and
over   your mouth

TONIGHT
quietness.   In me
and the room.

I am enclosed
by a thought

and some walls.

THE BRUISE

Again you have left
your mark.

Or we
have.

Skin shuddered
secretly

FLIES

tonight
in this room
two flies
on the ceiling
are making
love
quietly.   Or

so it seems
down here

YOUR BLOUSE

I people
this room
with things, a
chair, a lamp, a
fly   two books by
Marianne Moore.

I have thrown my
blouse on the floor.

Was it only
last night?

YOU
took

with so much
gentleness

my dark

Suite II

While you were away

I held you like this
in my mind.

It is a good mind
that can embody
perfection   with exactitude.

The sun comes through
plum curtains.

I said
the sun is gold

in your eyes.

It isn't the sun
you said.

On the floor your blouse.
The plum light
falls more golden

going down.

Tonight
quietness
in the room.

We knew

Then you must go.
I sat cross-legged
on the bed.
There is no room
for self-pity
I said

I lied

In the gold darkening
light

you dressed.

I hid my face
in my hair.

The room that held you

is still here

You brought me clarity.

Gift after gift
I wear.

Poems,   naked,

in the sunlight

on the floor.

Non Linear

An instant of white roses.
               Inbreathing.
A black butterfly's
             twitch and determined
collapse on a yellow round.

near the white Tanabe
narcissus
near Layton's *Love*
daffodils
outside   falling on
the pavement
the plum blossoms
of Cypress Street

the yellow chrysanthemums

      (I hide my head when I sleep)

a stillness
in jade

        (Your hand reaches out)

the chrysanthemums

are

        (Job's moaning, is it, the dark?)

a whirlwind!

Eros! *Agápe Agápe*

Her sickness does not ebb
anyhow, it's not a sea
it's a lake largely
      moon-ridden.

I can see her perfectly clearly
through this dusk her face
the colour of moonlight.

Maybe my body, maybe I?
But when has my love
          ever been
offered exactly
and why should she be an
            exception?

walking in dark

waking in dark the presence of all

the absences we have known.   Oceans.

so we are distinguished to ourselves

don't want that distinction.

I am afraid.   I said that.   I said that

for you.

My white skin
is not the moonlight.
If it is
tell me, who reads
by that light?

a curve / broken
of green
moss weed
kelp   shells   pebbles
lost orange rind
orange crab   pale
delicates at peace
on this sand
tracery of last night's
tide

I am listening for
the turn of the tide
I imagine it will sound
an appalled sigh
the sigh of Sisyphus
who was not happy

Hieratic sounds emerge
from the Priestess of
Motion
a new alphabet
gasps for air.

We disappear in the musk of her coming.

I hear the waves
hounding the window:
lord, they are the root waves
of the poem's meter
the waves of the
root poem's sex.
The waves of Event
(the major planets, the minor
planets, the Act)
break down at my window:
I also hear those waves.

the dead dog now
the one I saw last night
carried on a man's shoulders
down to the beach
he held it by its
dead crossed legs

I have given up
complaining

but nobody
notices

"That ye resist not
evil" falling
limp into the arms
of the oppressor
he is not undone
by the burden
of your righteousness
he has touched you

Suite of Lies

I know the way
of the pear tree
and apple tree the way
the light shines
through pear petal
apple, a light
falling into our
consanguinity

brother and   sister
conjunctive and
peaceable

I use the word groves
light falling
found in the orchard
finding what fell by a
breath

brother and sister
those children

the way of what fell
the lies
like the petals
falling   drop
delicately

Some final questions

What are you sad about?

that all my desire goes
out to the impossibly
beautiful

Why are you standing there staring?

I am watching a shadow
shadowing a shadow

Now you are sitting doubled up in pain.
What's that for?

doubled up I feel
small like these poems
the area of attack
is diminished

What do you really want?

want the apple on the bough in
the hand in the mouth seed
planted in the brain want
to think "apple"

*I don't get it. Are you talking about
process and individuation. Or absolutes
whole numbers that sort of thing?*

Yeah.

But why don't you do something?

I am trying to write a poem

Why?

Listen. If I have known beauty
let's say I came to it
asking

Oh?

STATEMENTS BY THE POETS

Robin Blaser

I'm grateful that for some "The Moth Poem" is a goody, but for me, it's also an oldy. Its date: 1962. It still interests me as one of the poems – serial and continuing – now to be gathered together in the collected *Holy Forest*. Especially for the moth in the piano early one morning and for that quick appearance and disappearance of the figuration of the priest-poet in the next to last poem – so little understood then. And for the wavering interruption of the music of the spheres – in a traditional notation. My thought of what may be aging in the poem is allayed by bpNichol's startling response to it in the spring of 1988 with his "Moth" poem. I have found in the serial poem a way to work from my displaced, uncentred "I" in order to be found among things – relational, at least, to what I can. Recent theory tells us writers that the author is gone from his / her authority. That seemed real enough to me before theory ever hit home. And, without authority, a conversation went on. When gathered in *The Holy Forest*, "The Moth Poem" will become only one movement among many. But *The Holy Forest* somehow isn't a book. I don't know how to write one anymore. The covers won't close. I asked a scholar and friend of these matters, "What do you say when asked about the serial poem and how it works?" Miriam Nichols answered, "The serial poem builds worlds that are provisional, and those worlds are specific, but not limited, in place and time – the result: plural worlds." So, I guess, "The Moth Poem," though back there, is still working at my initial sense of the multiplicity of times, persons, gods, things, thoughts, places and stuff – folding –

Biography

Robin Blaser was born in Denver, Colorado in 1925 and became a Canadian citizen in 1972. From: Twin Falls, Idaho; Evanston, Illinois; Caldwell, Idaho; Berkeley, California; Cambridge, Massachusetts; Paris; San Francisco. To: Vancouver, B.C. 1966. He retired, after twenty years to the day, from teaching at Simon Fraser University to work on his collected poems and collected essays – the poems to be called *The Holy Forest* and the essays, *Astonishments*.

By Robin Blaser

The Moth Poem. San Francisco: Open Space, 1964.
Les Chimères. San Francisco: Open Space, 1964.
Cups. San Francisco: Four Seasons, 1968.
"The Holy Forest Section." *Caterpillar* 12, 1970.
Image-Nation 1-12. London: Ferry, 1974.
Image-Nation 13 & 14. Vancouver: Cobblestone, 1975.
Syntax. Vancouver: Talon, 1983.
The Faerie Queene & The Park. Vancouver: Fissure, 1988.

Pell Mell. Toronto: Coach House, 1988.

About Robin Blaser

Nichols, Miriam. "Robin Blaser's *Syntax:* Performing the Real." *Line* 3 (Spring, 1984).
———. "Independent Realities: Notes on Robin Blaser's *Pell Mell.*" *Sulfur* 27 (Fall, 1990): 222-226.
———. "Robin Blaser's Poetics of Relation: Thinking Without Bannisters." *Sagetrieb,* forthcoming.
Owen, Judith. Review of *Syntax. Canadian Literature* 103 (Winter, 1984): 95-96.

George Bowering

Sometimes I agree with Edgar Allan Poe in his famous pronouncement that there is no such thing as a long poem. He said that even *Paradise Lost* is a number of short poems separated by prose passages.

Sometimes I think that in every long poem there is a short poem, trying to get out. Once in a while I think it goes the other way round.

In the early 1960s, I started a magazine expressly for long poems and shorter poems, because at that time there werent (m)any magazines that printed long poems. This is part of poetic history.

But I dont recall having held any great theories about the long poem. I know, I have heard, that the long poem is somehow normal to Canada. Well, Dryden me no Drydens, Pope me no Popes.

I noticed that in the United States all the good Modernist poets, all the Imagist poets, went ahead and made the long poem their main life's work. *The Cantos. The War Trilogy. Paterson. A. Lifting Belly.*

Then along came the poets of the New American Poetry, making the long poem their life's work. *The Maximus Poems. The Structure of Rime. Howl. Gunslinger.*

The Canadian poets got into the act. I do not mean E. J. Pratt, though you may. I mean the twentieth-century Canadian poets and their life's work. *The Second Scroll. Atlantis. Field Notes. Steveston. The Abbotsford Guide to India. Circe: Mud Poems. The Martyrology.*

In the twentieth century it became easy to write poems. More people knew how to write, and owned pencils. Free verse looked, to a lot of the newly literate, like something anyone could do. The world became a place in which anyone could find the time and words to produce short poems. Millions of short poems.

But still the long poem, I think, has always been the main activity of really serious poets. I mean I think that Robert Creeley's lifetime of slant views has been more like a long poem than it has been like the short poems we have come to associate with magazines like *Atlantic Monthly* and *The New Yorker*, where American poets without genius publish.

In the eighteenth century the important verse is found in long poems. Among the Romantics and the Victorians the reputations were made on long poems of heroic visionary voyages.

In schools these days, poetry is presented in the form of samplers, a few pages of him, a few lyrics of her. The long poem does not fare well in the normal textbook. Book-length poems are often not kept in print because they were published by literary presses rather than oil company diversifications.

Here in Canada, in the late twentieth century, anyway, the major form of poetry is just about invisible. So why do I keep writing long poems? Well, Barrie did. Bob does. Nicole does. This is how we talk to each other. We are so lonely otherwise. This is how we say our final important serious stuff to each other.

Biography

George Bowering was born in 1936 in Penticton, B.C. He attended Victoria College (Victoria, B.C.), the University of British Columbia, and the University of Western Ontario. He received his M.A. from U.B.C. in 1963. From 1954 to 1957 he was a photographer with the Royal Canadian Air Force. He has taught at several universities and colleges in Canada and the U.S. as well as in Rome and Berlin, and has been on the faculty of Simon Fraser University in Burnaby, B.C. since 1972. He has won the Governor General's Award twice, for poetry in 1969 and for fiction in 1980. He has published over twenty books of poetry, fiction and prose.

By George Bowering

Book-length Poems:
Sitting in Mexico. Calgary: Beaver Kosmos, 1965.
Baseball. Toronto: Coach House, 1967.
George, Vancouver. Kitchener: Weed/Flower, 1970.
Geneve. Toronto: Coach House, 1971.
Autobiology. Vancouver: New Star, 1972.
Curious. Toronto: Coach House, 1973.
At War with the U.S. Vancouver: Talon, 1974.
Allophanes. Toronto: Coach House, 1976.
Ear Reach. Vancouver: Alcuin, 1982.
Kerrisdale Elegies. Toronto: Coach House, 1984.

Dionne Brand

What I try to do in *No Language Is Neutral* is to make the poem sound like a constant and full humming. I intended it to be felt as a sustained rhythm and to engage itself in itself, using some of what Henry Louis Gates calls "Black rhetorical tropes ... 'marking,' 'loud talking,' 'specifying,' 'testifying,' 'calling out' (of one's name), 'sounding'...." Therefore I've tried to make the world over in the poems, spoken in what my grandmother used to call "womanish language." The structure of the lines came out of the need to say the thing. I wanted to fill every silence with a word and every word with a silence. Since there are so many silences to fill and so many words to silence, the poem continues.

Biography

Dionne Brand was born in Trinidad and has lived in Toronto for the past twenty years. She is a poet and writer, with a special interest in Black women's history and film, and has also published short stories and one work of non-fiction. She has been writer-in-residence at the Halifax Regional Library and at the University of Toronto.

By Dionne Brand

'Fore day morning. Toronto: Khoisan Artists, 1978.
Earth Magic. Toronto: KidsCan Press, 1979.
Primitive Offensive. Toronto: Williams-Wallace, 1982.
Winter Epigrams and *Epigrams to Ernesto Cardenal in Defense of Claudia.* Toronto: Williams-Wallace, 1983.
Chronicles of the Hostile Sun. Toronto: Williams-Wallace, 1984.
Rivers Have Sources Trees Have Roots: Speaking of Racism. Toronto: Cross Cultural Communication Centre, 1986.
Sans Souci and Other Stories. Stratford, Ont.: Williams-Wallace, 1988.
No Language Is Neutral. Toronto: Coach House, 1990.

Christopher Dewdney

A Natural History of Southwestern Ontario, of which *The Cenozoic Asylum* is Book Two, is a hyper-referential project, a compendium of particulars written from the inside of its subject. These particulars inventory a personal, regional identity directly informed by natural history. Many of the creatures, locales and weather conditions in this poem have their correlates around the globe, particularly in tropical regions.

Because *A Natural History of Southwestern Ontario* is a ritual text, each book has to be preceded by the first-hand account of someone who has been *inside* a tornado. This is a primal, sacred experience of nature's most extreme and random violence. However, it is a cruelty without malice derived from an impartiality at the heart of nature, and the universe for that matter. Ultimately our cosmos functions as an inhuman, yet intimate, phenomenology to which we impute deistic attributes because we cannot conceive of anything so subtle and complex as operating without consciousness as we know it.

Biography

Christopher Dewdney was born in London, Ontario in 1951. An active figure in the North American avantgarde, he has published eleven books of poetry, including, in 1986, *The Immaculate Perception*, a book about human consciousness and its relation to the brain as revealed by language, dreams and perception. In that same year he won first prize in the national CBC Literary Competition for poetry. In 1984, his selected poems, *Predators of the Adoration*, was nominated for the Governor General's Award, as were *The Immaculate Perception* in 1987 and *The Radiant Inventory* in 1989. He lives in Toronto where he teaches part-time at York University.

By Christopher Dewdney

Spring Trances in the Control Emerald Night: Book One of A Natural History of Southwestern Ontario. Berkeley: The Figures, 1978.
The Cenozoic Asylum: Book Two of A Natural History of Southwestern Ontario. Liverpool: Delires, 1983.
Predators of the Adoration: Selected Poems. Toronto: McClelland and Stewart, 1983.
The Immaculate Perception. Toronto: House of Anansi, 1986.
Permugenesis: A Recombinant Text: Book Three of A Natural History of Southwestern Ontario. Toronto: Nightwood, 1987.
The Radiant Inventory. Toronto: McClelland and Stewart, 1988.
Concordat Proviso Ascendants: Book Three of A Natural History of Southwestern Ontario. Great Barrington, Mass.: The Figures, 1991.

About Christopher Dewdney

Dragland, Stan. "Christopher Dewdney's Writing: Beyond Science and Madness." *The Malahat Review* 66 (October 1983); Reprinted in *The Bees of the Invisible.* Toronto: Coach House, 1991

Fawcett, Brian. "Dewdney's Poetic Method in *The Immaculate Perception*: A Conversation with Chris Dewdney." *Line* 9 (1987).

Highet, Alistair. "Manifold Destiny: Metaphysics in the Poetry of Christopher Dewdney." *Essays on Canadian Writing* 34 (Spring 1987).

McCaffery, Steve. "Strata and Strategy: Pataphysics in the Poetry of Christopher Dewdney." *Open Letter*, 3rd ser.4 (Winter 1976). (Reprinted in *North of Intention: Critical Writings 1973–1986.* New York: Roof; Toronto: Nightwood, 1986).

Louis Dudek

All my poetic development begins with the Imagist movement: with William Carlos Williams' "Red Wheelbarrow" etc.; and H.D. – especially early H.D. – whom I have admired greatly; and Richard Aldington, one of my preferred poets from early on; and Ezra Pound, of course, a little later than these. Imagism is the distillation of poetry into a short form, often visual, though it doesn't have to be visual. Imagism is the quintessence of poetry, so to speak, and also the quintessence of modernism, I should think, at least I have always said so.

But then I went on to write a long poem. And in the end I began to construct this long poem piecemeal, beginning with *En México*, and the poem "At Lac En Coeur" (1959), then going on to *Atlantis*, making it out of short poems, so that the short and the long come together somehow. In the long poem, inevitably, the technique of the short poem, of the Imagist poem, is what makes it possible.

The long poem cannot be a digressive, expansive, boring exposition. It is really made of very sharp, Imagistic, quintessential poetic elements. I believe that the great, wonderful, paradisal reality called "Atlantis" is not somewhere out there, not somewhere in the Provence or in ancient China, but is right here. It is in the actual, always changing and moving and transforming itself. And for that reason one has to get down to the everyday occurrence.

When I was writing *Europe*, I was quite aware that this was *not* a poem containing history in Pound's way, it was not a poem about the past; it is about the present. I was incorporating historical material from immediate experience, writing about the present condition of the world, and as a result the poem is shot through with historical insight and thought about history. I knew that it had an epic element also, that this big wind, running through the poem, is epic in kind. An epic mode is a larger emotion or idea that pushes along one poem after another, and then still another – it has momentum. It's very different from being suddenly moved to write a short poem. An epic is something larger, in theme and emotional power; I actually made the discovery, by experiencing it, that this might be possible, that something like it might be possible in the twentieth century.

However, there is a lot more to this. You see, after *The Transparent Sea* – I think it was in 1956 – I went to Mexico, to write *En México*, and there's obviously a great deal of dejection underlying that poem and that whole period of my poetry. And during that period, or a bit earlier, I wrote the short metrical poems that stand out in my poetry: the poetry of, you know, the mid-life crisis or whatever. Everyone has this kind of experience at some time in life, and for poets it goes with a certain kind of poem, which tends to be short and tends to be more traditional. Anyhow, getting out of that, I think, is what *En México* is all about, and also the long poems that follow. It's tied up, too, with world despair. *En México* is made of fragments for all those reasons. I'm coming out of something, and yet I'm getting those little sparks of light coming through. And euphoric passages. But you can see the kind of despair that underlies the poem. I mean, a kind of struggle against despair is probably true of my poetry through *En México, Atlantis* and *Continuation.* It's a personal condition – my special case – and yet today it wouldn't be possible for any poet to write significant poetry without something like that. We're all facing a very difficult time in history; but then humankind always has, I imagine. Maybe it's a universal condition.

The poem *En México* is fascinating in the way it got the form it has because at the time of writing I had no purpose in mind and there was nothing that I even vaguely proposed to myself as a subject. But I wrote down lines of poetry, fragments as they came, and these later became the poem. This method is something you will find developing gradually in my poetry, with hints of it even in obscure smaller poems. For instance, the poem "Artist's Life" in the Coach House book *Cross-Section* (also in *Infinite Worlds*). That poem is quite early: it was written sometime around 1948 in New York. And it already has this feeling of flow. The words are flowing through time, an actual record of one day, made of fragments of thought – so that it contains something of my later method. I thought at the time the poem was of no particular importance, but, with the years, I kept returning to it in memory as a touchstone.

From the time that I was, say, about eight or ten years old, I can remember a mode of feeling and consciousness that was all my own, which I knew was the way I saw things or felt things. Ultimately, the purpose must be to take that consciousness, which is always you, which is continuous and perhaps enriching itself with experience, and find a way of putting it down on paper. So essentially the form is the truth of your being: it must correspond to what actually is happening in the human mind.

– from an interview with Louise Shrier in *Zymergy*, Vol. 4, No. 2 (Autumn, 1990).

Biography

Louis Dudek is important among the pioneers of the Canadian long poem, for *Europe, En México, Atlantis* and *Continuation.* He received his doctorate at Columbia in New York. He has been active as a critic and modernist theoretician, and has influenced the teaching of poetry in Canadian schools and universities. Dudek has been an editor and publisher for over forty-five years. He was the founder of such magazines as *CIV/n* and *Delta*, and established Contact Press in Montreal and, with others, Delta Canada. Prior to his retirement, he was Greenshields Professor of English at McGill University.

By Louis Dudek

East of the City. Toronto: Ryerson, 1946.
The Searching Image. Toronto: Ryerson, 1952.
Europe. Toronto: Contact, 1954; Erin, Ontario: Porcupine's Quill, 1991.
The Transparent Sea. Toronto: Contact, 1956.

Laughing Stalks. Toronto: Contact, 1958.
En México. Toronto: Contact, 1958.
Atlantis. Montreal: Delta, 1967.
Collected Poems. Montreal: Delta, 1971.
Cross-Section: Poems 1940-1980. Toronto: Coach House, 1980.
Continuation 1. Montreal: Véhicule, 1981.
Zembla's Rocks. Montreal: Véhicule, 1986.
Infinite Worlds: The Poetry of Louis Dudek. Montreal: Véhicule, 1988.
Continuation 11. Montreal: Véhicule, 1990.
Small Perfect Things. Montreal: DC Books, 1991.

About Louis Dudek

Blaser, Robin. Introduction to *Infinite Worlds: The Poetry of Louis Dudek.* Montreal: Véhicule, 1988.
Davey, Frank. *Louis Dudek & Raymond Souster.* Vancouver: Douglas & McIntyre, 1980.
Davey, Frank, and bpNichol, eds. "Louis Dudek: Texts and Essays." *Open Letter,* 4th ser. 8/9 (1981).
Dudek, Louis. *Autobiographical Essay.* Detroit: Gale Research, 1991.
Stromberg-Stein, S. *Louis Dudek: A Biographical Introduction to His Poetry.* Ottawa: Golden Dog, 1983.

Diana Hartog

In the winter of 1987, I drove to the Southern California desert to stay alone in a shack, a narrow "ranch house" homesteaded in the thirties and now surrounded by a nature conservancy.

The first night – lying awake in a bed that sagged in the middle – I listened to the wind. No one had told me about the fault-line either: the San Andreas Fault, which ran north/south under the ridge it had pushed up in the backyard. There are no real "yards" in the desert. Fences look ridiculous around a house. It seems best and less foolish to simply admit the sand, for it blows, creeps and is washed in anyway over the sill. I remember Gerry Gilbert's advice about leaving the ends of poems open. In the desert, I propped the screen door open with a rock to keep it from banging in the wind.

My favourite story, told to me by my only neighbour (he was eighty at the time, a widower and sweet on me), was when he tumbled off the end of his father's wagon into a dry creek bed. He was only a baby, and remembers sitting among the stones of the creek bed howling but then he stopped to watch the mule's ears twitch. The good animal had paused, turning his head to look back.

Things get lost in the desert. I began to take long naps. You should always wear a hat. One afternoon I returned from a trip to town for groceries to be informed by my neighbour that some fellow, a writer, said his name was Barry Lopez, had been wandering around the conservancy; but had left.

To cope with the sky, I enrolled in a class on astronomy on Wednesday nights. The class held a "Star Party" at the top of a peak. It was cold, and windy. From vans and station wagons the telescopes were unloaded – fat-barrelled, or slim and long and elegant. Everyone had their favourite constellations, ones they felt close to. The moon that night was half concrete, grey and unutterably cold through the eye of the telescope; and half gold.

Into the second month of my stay my neighbour shyly confessed to saying a rosary for me on Thursdays and Sundays.

In his last letter, he wrote that he still does. My Catholic grandmother used to kneel in morning mass while the beads of her rosary slipped through her fingers, round and round and round, for however long, depending upon her sins, or the sins of others like her, or the state of her knees.

Biography

Diana Hartog was born in California and received a master's degree from San Francisco State University. She moved to Canada in 1970 with her husband and daughter. Since divorced, she now lives in New Denver, B.C. Her first book, *Matinee Light*, won the Gerald Lampert Memorial Award from the League of Canadian Poets; *Candy From Strangers* won the 1986 B.C. Book Prize for poetry.

By Diana Hartog

Matinee Light. Toronto: Coach House, 1983.
Candy From Strangers. Toronto: Coach House, 1986.

About Diana Hartog

Edwards, Brian. "Dis-closures: Diana Hartog's Surprises in Half-Light." *The Malahat Review* 83 (Summer 1988).

Kamboureli, Smaro. "Tropics of Love in Diana Hartog's Poetry." *The Malahat Review* 83 (Summer 1988).

Tostevin, Lola Lemire. "Diana Hartog's *Candy From Strangers*." *Brick*. (Winter, 1987).

Roy Kiyooka

an unprinted Obit from
the files of the Vancouver Sun:

at exactly 12.38 am on May 18th
a much beloved Pear Tree was toppled by
repeated gusts of alacritous wind ...
its once splendid crown splintered and
impaled upon a hitherto unvisited
lawn. we all stood at our bedroom windows
in our assorted night gowns   Awed!
to see its shattered trunk and a hitherto
unperceived hole in the night sky!

let all the birds without perch or
umbrella tell you about its unquiet feasts.

     'pied pear   i love you
pith/ stem/ seed/ unvoiced sun,'
   the poet cried: as something
in him died that night to reveal
   the midnight stars.

Doesn't any poet write a single work all his livelong life? Break it up into measurable units, call each unit a lyric – a stroke of magic or, if you wish, a telltale paragraph. The long or short hiatuses between each word don't matter. Some poems come suddenly like an intrepid November flood while others take years to accumulate the necessary grit. I've been rereading *A.B.C. The Alphabetization of the Popular Mind* by Ivan Illich and Barry Sanders, a succinct treatise on why we've all become the linguistic / political creatures we are. According to them, the Homeric tradition, which is preliterate, posits an uninterrupted narrative without an actual text. Like it's all covert with actual and stored experiences, and given the time and occasion, it becomes an actual speaking or singing out. What moves me, moves, serpent-wise, through the body of my speech is nothing, if not both the seminal body and the insensate breath's filial bequest.

Biography

Roy Kiyooka currently lives in Vancouver. He has moved a great deal, having lived in Vancouver, Regina, Calgary, Montreal, Naramata, and the Northwest Territories. He is a poet and multi-media artist, whose work is documented in

Kiyooka 25 Years, a catalogue produced by the Vancouver Art Gallery. *Pear Tree Pomes* was nominated for the Governor General's Award.

By Roy Kiyooka

Kyoto Airs. Vancouver: Periwinkle, 1964.
Nevertheless These Eyes. Toronto: Coach House, 1967.
StoneDGloves. Toronto: Coach House, 1970.
"The Eye in the Landscape." *B.C. Almanac Catalogue*. Vancouver: The National Film Board of Canada, 1970.
Transcanadaletters. Vancouver: Talon, 1975.
Fontainebleau Dream Machine. Toronto: Coach House, 1977.
Pear Tree Pomes. Toronto: Coach House, 1987.
"Pacific Windows." *Capilano Review* Ser.2, No.3 (Fall 1990).

Robert Kroetsch

The long poem is the crack in the glaze that goes by the name of literature. The long poem tells us that underneath the glaze is the exquisite clay that we call writing. Birds, walking along the edges of rivers, taught us to write.

The long poem, nowadays, is the talk of various discourses with each other. The singing talker.

Somewhere in this poem I look into Homer's blind eyes and kiss the sound of his absent voice.

Delphi: Commentary is a devotional poem, in praise of daughters. This poem is a thanks poem for my father who, from the underworld, called me again to my task and my joy.

The long poem is the unstable subject speaking its exquisite and erotic becoming against the kangaroo courts of the poetic desire machine.

Biography

Robert Kroetsch was born in the Battle River country of Alberta in 1927. After working for six years in the Canadian North he went to the U.S. to enter graduate school. He taught at the State University of New York at Binghamton for seventeen years before moving to the University of Manitoba. His seven novels include *The Studhorse Man, Badlands,* and *What the Crow Said.* He won the Governor General's Award for Fiction in 1969. His mosaic long poem, written over a period of fifteen years, was collected in 1989 under the title *Completed Field Notes.* "Delphi: Commentary" is part of that mosaic. *The Lovely Treachery of Words,* the first volume of his anti-autobiographical diptych, also appeared in 1989.

By Robert Kroetsch

The Studhorse Man. Toronto: Macmillan of Canada, 1969.
Badlands. Toronto: New Press, 1975.
Stone Hammer Poems. Lantzville: Oolichan, 1975.
Seed Catalogue. Winnipeg: Turnstone, 1977.
What the Crow Said. Don Mills: General Publishing, 1978.
The Sad Phoenician. Toronto: Coach House, 1979.
Alibi. Toronto: General Publishing, 1983.
Advice to My Friends. Don Mills: General Publishing, 1985.
Excerpts from the Real World. Lantzville: Oolichan, 1986.
Completed Field Notes. Toronto: McClelland and Stewart, 1989.
The Lovely Treachery of Words. Toronto: Oxford, 1989.

Daphne Marlatt

These poems of presence were largely written out of absence. Their matrix was an exchange of letters and poems, in the late summer and fall of 1982, with the woman who was, and is, my partner Betsy Warland. Except for the last three poems, each was written through the ache of distance, by the light of memory, and in the heat of our writing back and forth to each other as i drove east to Winnipeg where i spent several months. The last three were written back on the coast after i had rejoined her, although they too talk of separation, other forms of it.

But these biographical factors are also completely inessential because the poems witness the mobility of time and place in the immanence of a language invoked by desire. A calling to, becomes a calling up, becomes a calling into speech of the unspeakable. Memory, it turns out, is an open vehicle we also move in. And an "act" of memory-speech translates us, carries us across, from there to here.

In its original Longspoon edition, *Touch to My Tongue* was joined by photographs from Cheryl Sourkes's sequence, "Memory Room." A collaboration of ideas. Betsy's sequence of poems which forms the other half of our exchange, "Open is Broken," can be found in her collection of the same name (Longspoon, 1984).

Biography

West Coast writer Daphne Marlatt is the author of a number of books of poetry and/or prose including *Touch to My Tongue, How Hug a Stone, What Matters,* and *Steveston.* Her most recent publications are a novel, *Ana Historic,* and a poetic collaboration with Betsy Warland, *Double Negative.* She has been a contributing editor for *West Coast Review, Island, The Capilano Review* and *Tish* and an editor for *periodics* magazine. She is a founding member of the feminist editorial collective *Tessera,* a twice-yearly journal of new Quebecoise and English-Canadian feminist theory and writing. She makes her home on Salt Spring Island, where she is currently working on a new collection of poetry titled *Salvage.*

By Daphne Marlatt

Steveston. Vancouver: Talon, 1974; Edmonton: Longspoon, 1984.
How Hug a Stone. Winnipeg: Turnstone, 1983.
Touch to My Tongue. Edmonton: Longspoon, 1984.
With Betsy Warland. *Double Negative.* Charlottetown: Gynergy, 1988.
Ana Historic. Toronto: Coach House, 1988.
With Sky Lee, Lee Maracle and Betsy Warland, eds. *Telling It: Women and Language Across Cultures.* Vancouver: Press Gang, 1990.

About Daphne Marlatt

On *Touch to My Tongue:*
Banting, Pamela. "Powers of Seduction." *Prairie Fire* VII, 3.
Bennett, Donna. "Their Own Tongue," *Canadian Literature* 107, Winter 1985.
Dragland, Stan. (Untitled). *Journal of Canadian Poetry* I; Reprinted in revised form as " 'Creatures of Ecstacy': *Touch to my Tongue*" in *Bees of the Invisible,* Toronto: Coach House, 1991
Fitzgerald, Judith. "Women's vision comes of age." *The Toronto Star* (February 24, 1985).
Godard, Barbara. "Body I: Daphne Marlatt's Feminist Poetics." *The American Book Review* XV, 4 (Winter 1985).
McLaren, Juliet. (Untitled). *B.C. Library Association Reporter* (January 1985).
Mouré, Erin. (Untitled). *Books in Canada* (October 1985).
Parks, Joy. "Breaking taboos." *Herizons* III, 2 (March 1985).

On *Ana Historic:*
Dragland, Stan. "Out of the Blank: Daphne Marlatt's *Ana Historic*" in *Bees of the Invisible,* Toronto: Coach House, 1991

Interviews:

Williamson, Janice. "Speaking in and of Each Other." *Fuse* VII, 5 (February/March 1985).
Wright, Ellea. "Text and Tissue: Body Language." *Broadside* VI, 3 (December 1984/January 1985).

David McFadden

A poem is a small painting, a long poem is a mural. For thirty years I have been obsessed with writing long poems that make use of a form that has been designed specifically for that poem before a word of the poem has been written and without benefit of any idea of what is going to be going on in the poem once the writing begins. When I design the form the poem is going to take, using Cage-like random operations, there is a sense of exhilaration, as if I am a painter stretching a canvas. I've always envied painters.

What is primarily enviable about painters is their canvases or other surfaces. A painter always knows the shape and dimension of the painting before he begins painting and a poet seldom has access to this sort of convenience.

Knowing the shape and dimensions of a canvas or other surface beforehand liberates the painter from numerous miscellaneous agonies. Nothing liberates the poet. Many a mind was lost for lack of a canvas to stretch.

Biography

Born in Hamilton, Ontario, in 1940, David McFadden has written more than a dozen books of poetry, five novels and one collection of short stories. A former newspaper reporter, he taught at the David Thompson University Centre for three years, during which time he founded the magazine *Writing* and edited the first five issues, and has been writer-in-residence at Simon Fraser University, the University of Western Ontario, the Metropolitan Toronto Public Library and the Hamilton Public Library. Three of his books – *On the Road Again, The Art of Darkness* and *Gypsy Guitar* – were nominated for Governor General's Awards. He lives in Toronto.

By David McFadden

The Poem Poem. Kitchener, Ont.: Weed/Flower, 1967.
Letters from the Earth to the Earth. Toronto: Coach House, 1968.
The Saladmaker. Montreal: Imago, 1968. (Revised edition, Montreal: Cross Country, 1977.)
Poems Worth Knowing. Toronto: Coach House, 1971.
Intense Pleasure. Toronto: McClelland and Stewart, 1972.
The Ova Yogas. Toronto: Ganglia and Weed/Flower, 1972.
The Great Canadian Sonnet. Toronto: Coach House, 1975.
A Knight in Dried Plums. Toronto: McClelland and Stewart, 1975.
The Poet's Progress. Toronto: Coach House, 1977.
I Don't Know. Montreal: Cross Country, 1977.
On the Road Again. Toronto: McClelland and Stewart, 1978.
A New Romance. Montreal: Cross Country, 1979.

My Body Was Eaten by Dogs: Selected Poems. Toronto: McClelland and Stewart, 1981; New York: Cross Country, 1981.
A Trip around Lake Erie. Toronto: Coach House, 1981.
A Trip around Lake Huron. Toronto: Coach House, 1981.
Country of the Open Heart. Edmonton: Longspoon, 1982.
Three Stories and Ten Poems. Toronto: Identity, 1982.
Animal Spirits: Stories to Live By. Toronto: Coach House, 1983.
A Pair of Baby Lambs. Toronto: Front, 1983.
The Art of Darkness. Toronto: McClelland and Stewart, 1984.
Canadian Sunset. Windsor: Black Moss; Toronto: Firefly, 1986.
Gypsy Guitar. Vancouver: Talon, 1987.
A Trip around Lake Ontario. Toronto: Coach House, 1988

About David McFadden

Czarnecki, Mark. "Believing Is Seeing." *Books in Canada* (January 1987).
Doyle, James. "McFadden's World." *Canadian Literature* 120 (Spring 1989).
Draper, Gary. "Interview with David McFadden." *Books in Canada* (October 1984).
Fawcett, Brian. "McFadden's Dilemma." *Books in Canada* (March 1987).
————. "No Harp Music." *Books in Canada* (May 1988).
French, William. "Freshwater Ulysses." *Globe and Mail* (November 26, 1988).
Jirgens, Karl. "McFadden's Gypsy Poems." *Essays on Canadian Writing* 40 (Spring 1990).
Lamenza, Lavinia. "Objectify Everything: An Interview with David McFadden." *Brick* 34 (Fall 1988).
Lillard, Rhonda Batchelor. "On David McFadden's *Gypsy Guitar.*" *Brick* 34 (Fall 1988).
McCarthy, Dermot. "The Dying Generations." *Essays on Canadian Writing* 28 (Spring 1987).
Morrissey, Stephen. "Seven Day Quest." *Matrix* 29 (Fall 1989).
Nichol,bp. "David McFadden's Art of Darkness." *Brick* 28 (Fall 1986).
Thompson, Kent. "Zinging Them In." *Books in Canada* (April 1989).

Barry McKinnon

In the spring of 1970 while revising a short, unfinished poem, I sensed that the subject was too large for the kind of lyric I was in the habit of writing. The urgency, impulse and push of its untold story kept me writing steadily for the next three weeks. The route this little fragment opened seemed to say: you can sum up your life to this point *if you keep at it*. Yet, I was afraid that this emerging long poem with its complex set of elements and conditions (fragments, images, ideas, memories, *and* a series of photographs, etc.) would fail and end nowhere. The pleasure of the writing, however, was to be in a poem with such a large context of space and time – to be in a form that, paradoxically, gave me new energy and confidence, I didn't know what I was doing but I was doing it. The result was the book-length poem, *I Wanted to Say Something*.

Since then I've been writing the long poem / serial sequence, a form that gives me the necessary range in which to articulate the poem's central truth from various and variable angles and perspectives. I see the long poem, also, as a way to log my experience *and* to record what I value most in a context of forces, subtle or not, that threaten those values. As D. H. Lawrence writes: "We've got to live no matter how many skies have fallen." I believe the poem helps us build up "new little habitats" in the detritus and helps us live because it also contains our affirmation, hope and joy.

Biography

I was born in 1944 in Calgary, Alberta where I grew up. In 1965, after two years of college, I attended Sir George Williams University in Montreal and took two courses with Irving Layton before graduating in 1967 with a B.A. I graduated in 1969 with an M.A. from U.B.C. and was hired to teach English at the College of New Caledonia in Prince George where I've been ever since. The real biography, needless to say, is in the poems.

By Barry McKinnon

The Golden Daybreak Hair. Toronto: Aliquondo, 1967.
The Carcasses of Spring. Vancouver: Talon, 1971.
The Death of a Lyric Poet. Prince George: Caledonia Writing Series, 1975.
Songs & Speeches. Prince George: Caledonia Writing Series, 1976.
I Wanted to Say Something. Prince George: Caledonia Writing Series, 1976.
Sex at Thirty-One. Prince George: Caledonia Writing Series, 1977.
The the. (Fragments.) Prince George: Caledonia Writing Series, 1977.
The the. Toronto: Coach House, 1980.
Thoughts/Sketches. Prince George: Tatlow; Vancouver: Gorse, 1985.
The Centre. Burnaby: Line Up One. *Line: A Journal of Contemporary Writing and its Modernist Sources,* 1985.

bpNichol

When we write as we write we are always telling a story. When I write as I write I am telling the story of how I see the world, how it's been given to me, what I take from it. In the long poem I have the time to tell you that in all its faces or, at least, in as many faces as I've seen so far. Even when I'm not telling a specific story, I'm telling you *that* story. A narrative in language. The long poem. How I see the world.
– from "Narrative in Language: The Long Poem"; *The Dinosaur Review,* reprinted in *Tracing the Paths.* Vancouver: Line/Talon, 1988.

Biography

bpNichol wrote eleven books of poetry, four novels, several children's books and one collection of short fiction. He was recognized internationally as a writer, particularly as a poet. He produced in his lifetime many pamphlets, broadsides, and other ephemera, as well as records and tapes of his readings both alone and with the sound poetry ensemble The Four Horsemen. bpNichol won the Governor General's Award for Poetry in 1970. He is the subject of Michael Ondaatje's film *Sons of Captain Poetry* and is in Ron Mann's film *Poetry in Motion. The Martyrology,* bpNichol's lifework, is regarded as a major poetic achievement.

By bpNichol

Journeying & the Returns. Toronto: Coach House, 1967.
The Martyrology, Books 1 and 2. Toronto: Coach House, 1972.
The Martyrology, Books 3 and 4. Toronto: Coach House, 1976.
The Martyrology, Book 5. Toronto: Coach House, 1982.
Zygal: A Book of Mysteries & Translations. Toronto: Coach House, 1985.
The Martyrology, Book 6 Books. Toronto: Coach House, 1987.
gifts: The Martyrology Book(s) 7 &. Toronto: Coach House, 1990.
Art Facts. Tucson: Chax, 1990.

About bpNichol

Miki, Roy, ed. *Tracing the Paths: Reading ≠ Writing The Martyrology.* Vancouver: Line/Talon, 1988

Michael Ondaatje

Margaret Avison has said that literature results when "every word is written in the full light of *all* a writer knows." The long poem shows a process of knowledge, of discovery during the actual writing of the poem. "You have to go into a serial poem not knowing what the hell you're doing," wrote Jack Spicer. The poets do not fully know what they are trying to hold until they near the end of the poem, and this uncertainty, this lack of professional intent, is what allows them to go deep. The poems have more to do with open fields and quiet rooms than public stages.... These poets listen to everything. Kroetsch hangs around bars picking up stories like Polonius behind the curtain, others recall childhood language, or hold onto dreams after they have awakened, or speak the unsaid politics of the day. They tempt quiet things out of the corner. "It is not easy to catch dogs when it is your business to catch dogs," said Steinbeck.– from the Introduction to *The Long Poem Anthology*.

Biography

Michael Ondaatje is a poet, novelist and film maker who lives in Toronto where he teaches at Glendon College, York University. He has twice won the Governor General's Award for poetry. His prose works include *Coming Through Slaughter*, *Running in the Family*, *The Collected Works of Billy the Kid* and *In the Skin of a Lion*. He is also the editor of *From Ink Lake*, an anthology of Canadian stories.

By Michael Ondaatje

Books:
The Dainty Monsters. Toronto: Coach House, 1967.
The Man with Seven Toes. Toronto: Coach House, 1969.
Leonard Cohen. Toronto: McClelland and Stewart, 1969.
The Broken Ark. Ottawa: Oberon, 1969; reprinted as *A Book of Beasts*. Oberon, 1980.
The Collected Works of Billy the Kid. Toronto: House of Anansi, 1970.
Rat Jelly. Toronto: Coach House, 1973
Coming Through Slaughter. Toronto: House of Anansi, 1976.
The Long Poem Anthology. Toronto: Coach House, 1979.
There's a Trick with a Knife I'm Learning to Do. Toronto: McClelland and Stewart, 1979.
Elimination Dance. Ilderton, Ont.: Brick, 1979.
Tin Roof. Lantzville: Island, 1982.
Running in the Family. Toronto: McClelland and Stewart, 1982.
Secular Love. Toronto: Coach House, 1984.
In the Skin of a Lion. Toronto: McClelland and Stewart, 1988.
From Ink Lake. Toronto: Lester and Orpen Dennys, 1990.

Films:
Sons of Captain Poetry (a film on bpNichol). 1970.
Carry on Crime and Punishment. 1970.
The Clinton Special (a film on Theatre Passe Muraille's "The Farm Show"). 1980.
Love Clinic. 1991.

Lola Lemire Tostevin

It seems a misnomer to refer to the small poems of *Gyno-Text* as a long poem, yet the concept behind its development reflects what is usually perceived through the long poem: process and perspective.

Gyno-Text is an extended metaphor for a thirty-seven week pregnancy but these small poems are not about the mystification or sacred calling of motherhood. While pregnant with both my children, I followed in a medical textbook the process that the embryo or foetus undergoes at any specific time and while that was fascinating enough at a biological level, I found myself even more fascinated by the language and the images conveyed which had nothing to do with what was happening inside my body. I jotted down a few of the images, played around with the new words, then put everything aside and forgot about them. I was not yet thinking of myself as a writer.

It was a few years later when I lived in France during the seventies when so many various new theories around poetic language were being developed that I returned to these small poems. Almost everything I read around the language of poetry referred to *process, gestation*. I revelled in Julia Kristeva's concepts of *phéno-texte* and *géno-texte* that describe the main features of poetic language: phenotext as the familiar language of communication and genotext which operates at a level which doesn't necessarily reflect normal structures but generates elements of language in process. A sprouting which develops slowly as a seed and affords the writer a source of generative creative power. It is against this background that *Gyno-Text* was conceived. At the ridge where becoming of the subject is affirmed and developed through language in process.

Since the writing of this first book, I have considered all my collections of poems as long poems, each poem, each book but a different stage in a process through which different perspectives wait to be discovered.

Biography

Born in Timmins, Ontario into a French-Canadian family, Lola Lemire Tostevin currently lives in Toronto where she teaches creative writing at York University. She is married and has two children. Her published works include four collections of poetry and more than fifty reviews, essays, articles and translations.

By Lola Lemire Tostevin

Color of Her Speech. Toronto: Coach House, 1982.
Gyno-Text. Toronto: Underwich, 1983.
Double Standards. Edmonton: Longspoon, 1985.
'sophie. Toronto: Coach House, 1988.

Fred Wah

Length in poetry seems useful as a means by which to investigate the possibilities of a content, formally and, further, to extend the inquiry into contiguous aspects of the content. Such a process of composition offers generative resources that extend the dynamics of the poem (rhythm, repetition, shape, etc.) that not so much avoid cadence as configure it in different ways (cadence as shapely settling, not closure).

As well, the "long poem" offers more of that democratic dialogue currently in favour in writing. That is, the insistence of sub-, supra-, or alter-texts is much more likely given size.

"This Dendrite Map," for example, attempts to engage, in each separate piece, the reaction and resonance of the "haiku" that settles out at the bottom. These were interesting pieces to write because, while writing the prose, I was conscious of the word-rumble further down the line. Other than that, the relationship in this poem seems to be serial.

Six or seven years later I'm still spurred by the same content. For me the advantage of the long poem is the continuing biotext it affords – long poem, long life.

Biography

Fred Wah was born in Swift Current, Saskatchewan, in 1939, but grew up in the West Kootenay region of British Columbia. He studied music and English literature at the University of British Columbia in the early 1960s, where he was one of the founding editors of the poetry newsletter *TISH*. He did graduate work in literature and linguistics at the University of New Mexico in Albuquerque, where he edited *Sum* magazine. In 1967 he graduated with a master's degree from the State University of New York at Buffalo where he co-edited the *Niagara Frontier Review* and *The Magazine of Further Studies*. He returned to the Kootenays in the late 1960s and from there he edited *Scree*. He is currently a contributing editor of *Open Letter*. He has taught at Selkirk College and was the founding coordinator of the writing program at David Thompson University Centre. He now teaches at the University of Calgary. *Waiting for Saskatchewan* was awarded the Governor General's Award for Poetry in 1986. He has also written critiques of contemporary Canadian and American literature and is presently working on a verse-novel.

By Fred Wah

Lardeau. Toronto: Island, 1965.
Mountain. Buffalo: Audit, 1967.
Among. Toronto: Coach House, 1972.
Tree. Vancouver: Vancouver Community Press, 1972.
Earth. Canton: Institute of Further Studies, 1974.
Pictograms from the Interior of B.C. Vancouver: Talon, 1980.

Loki Is Buried at Smoky Creek: Selected Poetry. Vancouver: Talon, 1980.
Owners Manual. Lantzville: Island Writing Series, 1981.
Breathin' My Name with a Sigh. Vancouver: Talon, 1981.
Grasp the Sparrow's Tail. Kyoto, 1982.
Waiting for Saskatchewan. Winnipeg: Turnstone, 1985.
Rooftops. Maine: Blackberry, 1987; Red Deer: Red Deer College Press, 1988.
Music at the Heart of Thinking. Red Deer: Red Deer College Press, 1988.
Limestone Lakes Utaniki. Red Deer: Red Deer College Press, 1989.

About Fred Wah

Banting, Pamela. "The Undersigned: Ethnicity and Signature-Effects in Fred Wah's Poetry." *West Coast Line,* 2, (Fall 1990).
———. "Fred Wah: poet as theor(h)et(or)ician." *Open Letter,* 6th ser. 7 (1987).
Nichol, bp, and Pauline Butling. "Transcreation: A Conversation with Fred Wah: TRG Report one: Translation (Part 3)." *Open Letter,* 3rd ser. 9 (1978).
Kamboureli, Smaro. "Fred Wah: A Poetry of Dialogue." *Line* 4 (1984).
McCaffery, Steve. "Anti-Phonies." *Open Letter,* 6th ser. 2/3 (1985).
Munton, Ann. "The Long Poem as Poetic Diary." *Open Letter,* 6th ser. 5/6 (1986).
Scobie, Stephen. "Surviving the Paraph-raise." *Open Letter,* 6th ser. 5/6 (1986).
Tostevin, Lola Lemire. "Music, Heart, Thinking: An Interview with Fred Wah." *Line* 12 (1988).
Wah, Fred. "Making Strange Poetics." *Open Letter,* 6th ser. 2/3 (1985).

Phyllis Webb

When I speak of long lines and short lines I am not merely thinking of the effect of the line on the page, of its typographical effect – in fact, that is probably secondary. I am thinking of the phrasing, of the measure of the breath, of what is natural to the phrase, and one of my efforts in writing the small *Naked Poems* was first of all to clarify my statements so that I could see what my basic rhythms were; how I *really* speak, how my feelings come out on the page.

The *Naked Poems*, as I call them, are attempts to get away from a dramatic rhythm, from a kind of dramatic structure in the poem itself, *and* away from the metaphor very often, so that they are very bare, very simple. In a suite like this where the image is not realized in terms of metaphor, but is simply named, the *thing* is named – like the room, the plum colour, the curtains and the gold colour. These are not in effect metaphors but they have a kind of image-like impact as they build up through the two suites. And like the various kinds of rhyme I use in the poem, they too seem to me to have linking effect and are part of what I'd call the total music of the poem.

In these short poems I find that I run into all sorts of difficulties, one of which is sentence structure; that is, I find that the basic sentence structure is based on an opposition of ideas, so that you get "buts" and "thoughs" and "althoughs," or "ifs," and so on. And it seemed to me that this had some philosophical significance and that I had to break through the basic oppositions that are presented to us in everyday thought and get to a more refined synthesis. Well, I haven't arrived at this yet, but this is *one* of the intellectual problems, and one of the poetic problems.
– from "Polishing Up the View" in *Talking*.

Biography

Phyllis Webb was born and raised in Victoria, and now lives on Salt Spring Island, B.C. She has published ten collections of poetry and won the Governor General's Award in 1982 for *The Vision Tree*. Her most recent book is *Hanging Fire*.

By Phyllis Webb

Trio. Montreal: Contact, 1954 (with Gael Turnbull and Eli Mandel).
Even Your Right Eye. Toronto: McClelland and Stewart, 1956.
The Sea Is Also a Garden. Toronto: Ryerson, 1962.
Naked Poems. Vancouver: Periwinkle, 1965.
Selected Poems 1954-1965. Vancouver: Talon, 1971.
Wilson's Bowl. Toronto: Coach House, 1980.
Talking. Montreal: Quadrant, 1982.
Sunday Water: Thirteen Anti Ghazals. Lantzville: Island, 1982.
The Vision Tree: Selected Poems. Vancouver: Talon, 1982.

Water and Light: Ghazals and Anti-Ghazals. Toronto: Coach House, 1984.
Hanging Fire. Toronto: Coach House, 1990.

About Phyllis Webb

Butling, Pauline. "Paradox and play in the poetry of Phyllis Webb." *A Mazing Space: Writing Canadian Women Writing,* eds. Shirley Neuman and Smaro Kamboureli. Edmonton: NeWest, 1987.

Frey, Cecelia. "The Left Hand of Webb." *Prairie Fire* 7 (Autumn 1986).

————. "Phyllis Webb: An Annotated Bibliography." *The Annotated Bibliography of Canada's Major Authors,* eds. Robert Lecker and Jack David. Toronto: ECW, 1985.

Hulcoop, John. Introduction to *Selected Poems 1954-1965.* By Phyllis Webb. Vancouver: Talon, 1971.

————. "Phyllis Webb." *Dictionary of Literary Biography,* 53: *Canadian Writers Since 1960 First Series,* ed. W. H. New. Detroit: Bruccoli, 1986.

————. "Phyllis Webb and the Priestess of Motion." *Canadian Literature* 32 (Spring 1967).

Mallinson, Jean. "Ideology and Poetry: An Examination of Some Recent Trends in Canadian Criticism." *Studies in Canadian Literature* 3 (Winter 1978).

Mandel, Ann. "The Poetry of Last Things." *Essays on Canadian Writing* 26 (Summer 1983).

Woodcock, George. *Northern Spring: The Flowering of Canadian Literature.* Vancouver: Douglas and McIntyre, 1987.

Sharon Thesen is a poet, editor and critic whose selected poems, *The Pangs of Sunday,* was published by McClelland and Stewart in 1990. Her long poem for Malcolm Lowry, *Confabulations,* was published in 1982 by Oolichan Books. Poetry collections published by Coach House are *Artemis Hates Romance, Holding the Pose* and *The Beginning of the Long Dash.*

Editor for the Press: Michael Ondaatje
Cover Design: Shari Spier / Reactor

COACH HOUSE PRESS
401 (rear) Huron Street
Toronto, Canada M5S 2G5